IT Jobs Formula

The 1500+ Roles in IT and Where to Find Them
Fast

https://itjobsformula.com/

Matthew Bulat

M.Eng.Tech MACS

DEDICATION

For my wife, Paula, and children, Charlotte and Georgia.

CONTENTS

Matthew Bulat

Matthew Bulat

1 THE IT JOBS FORMULA ADVANTAGE

- Find more suitable IT Role titles within a day with 1500+ choices. Imagine more career possibilities.

- Know the IT Role phrase styles used by employers which means more job search queries and more job search results

- Quickly link to more global job opportunities including remote work possibilities. 1800+ direct IT Role links are supplied.

- Minimum and maximum salaries for 250+ IT roles on Seek are provided for your career planning

- Spend less time searching for jobs and more time applying for IT Roles

- Suitable for first job, career upgrade, career transition, contract work, project work or part time work

- IT Roles can be found in most industries which means more opportunities

1

- Some IT Roles can be performed from home remotely from the employer or client which means no commute

- Data from 6 job websites and 60,000 keywords were analysed to find the top 1500+ global unique IT Roles. The hard work is done for you.

- IT Jobs popularity by Internet traffic is provided for the 6 job websites. Keep your skills current with job trends.

- Free digital tools are provided to make your job search and find even faster

- How much time and effort can you save with your job search?

- Consider the value of finding your next ideal role sooner and being paid sooner

2 INTRODUCTION

"Employment of computer and information technology occupations is projected to grow 12 percent from 2018 to 2028, much faster than the average for all occupations. These occupations are projected to add about 546,200 new jobs." USA Bureau of Labor Statistics https://www.bls.gov/ooh/computer-and-information-technology/home.htm

"This 2019 edition forecasts that demand for technology workers will grow by 100,000 between 2018 and 2024 in trend terms" Australia Digital Pulse 2019.
https://www2.deloitte.com/au/en/pages/economics/articles/australias-digital-pulse.html

IT Jobs has an awareness problem, lots of available roles but low knowledge of the opportunities. The growth of the IT industry is causing pain in keeping up with the diversity of information and technology roles.

This book shows 1500+ unique IT Jobs from 6 job websites to solve this problem. You may be surprised on the number of IT Roles that are suitable to your needs. Career planning can be performed from junior to senior roles.

Using this book provides you with more suitable IT Role titles, more job search results and links directly to global job listings. This means quick access to extra appropriate job listings which can be applied for. Further benefits include a range of roles that can be performed remotely with global clients or employers.

The need for this books' knowledge can be tracked over 6 years where I have tracked the IT skills gap in Australia. For 6 years I have tracked the IT job demand on Seek which has managed to be the 1st, 2nd or 3rd in ranking industry in terms of total job vacancies. The industry sector job vacancy trend data was shown to job seekers at Career Expo events. Feedback from students show a low understanding on the IT job sector demand. In terms of IT role lists, Australian Computer Society Career Wheel shows 50 roles which is limiting. https://www.careersfoundation.com.au/ From 2013, I analyzed Elance (now Upwork) to list 200 IT roles used in $3B in IT projects. https://www.matthewb.id.au/career/worldwide-ICT-skills-demand.html While lecturing Internet Applications, an assignment question, "What are your views about the application development in the next few years?" prompted a proper response. SEMrush website analysis was done on 6 job websites to extract the top 10,000 keywords from each. IT roles data was extracted from each job website and then combined to deliver 1500+ unique IT roles. 7 web pages were created to support this book. https://itjobsformula.com/

3 HOW TO USE THIS BOOK

- Make a short list of IT roles you like from the list of 1500+. Look for alternate phrasing for similar roles.
- Search for the role in the 6 job website chapters, Seek, Indeed, Indeed UK, Freelancer, Upwork and Zip Recruiter
- 1800+ links are provided directly to job search results. The same links are also present from the digital tools.
- Apply for your dream IT Jobs

4 OPTIONAL EXTRA IT ROLE RESEARCH AND ACTIVITIES

- Note which companies employ your IT role
- Note the popular skills required for the role
- Look up the role in LinkedIn to find role examples
- Note the education and career paths to the role
- Consider following or connecting with persons of interest
- Follow the companies of interest
- Perform training for the role requirements if required
- Update your LinkedIn profile to complete All Star status including courses and skills
- Consider gaining experience in Freelancer or Upwork with short term projects

5 THE 1500+ ROLES IN IT – MAKE YOUR SUITABLE IT ROLES SHORTLIST

Highlight or note down the IT Roles that are suitable for you. Look for similar roles phrased differently. The more roles selected will lead to more job search queries and links in the next stage of your job search. The digital tool for this chapter is https://itjobsformula.com/jobs/ Export your IT Roles shortlist.

2d Animation Freelance Work, 2d Animation Work From Home, 3d Animation Work, 3d Architectural Visualization Freelance Jobs, 3d Artist Jobs, 3d Conversion Jobs, 3d Design Jobs Online, 3d Freelance Jobs Online, 3d Modelling Jobs, 3d Modelling Work At Home, 3d Outsourcing Jobs, 3d Rendering Jobs For Freelancers, 3d Visualizer Freelance Jobs, 3ds Max Designer Jobs, 3ds Max Freelance Work, 3ds Max Modelling Jobs, ABAP Freelance Opportunities, ABAP Jobs, Access Database Developer Freelance, Access VBA Developer, Active Directory Administrator, Ad Posting Jobs, Admin Online, Adobe After Effects Freelance, Adobe InDesign Jobs, Adobe Photoshop Freelance Work, AdSense Jobs Online, Affiliate Marketing Jobs, After Effects Freelance Work, Agile Business Analyst, Ai Freelance Jobs, Always Video Gaming, Amazon Com, Analyst Jobs, Analytical Skills, Analytics Projects Freelance, Android App Development Freelance Projects, Android App Development Online Jobs, Android Developer, Angular 2 Developer, Angular 2 Freelance Jobs, Angular Freelance Jobs, Animation Illustration Jobs, Animation Jobs, Animation Studios, Animation Work, Ansys Freelance, API Integration Jobs, App Developer Jobs, App Development Freelance Jobs, App

Promotion Jobs, App Testing Jobs Online, Apple Certified Mac Technician Jobs, Apple Store, ArcGIS Freelance Jobs, ArcGIS Online Jobs, Arduino Freelance Jobs, Arduino Jobs, Article Rewriting Jobs Online, Artificial Intelligence Freelance, Asp Net Developer, Asp Net Freelance Jobs, Asp Net MVC Freelance Jobs, Assistant Development Manager Brisbane, Assistant It Manager, Associate Business Analyst, Associates Degree In Computer Networking Jobs, Audio Engineering Jobs, AutoCAD Freelance Online, Autodesk Fusion Jobs, Autodesk Inventor Freelance Projects, Autodesk Inventor Work From Home, Automation Freelance, Automation Project Engineer Job Description, Aws Freelance Work, Aws Remote Jobs, Azure Consultant Jobs, Azure Freelance Jobs, Backend Freelance, Bash Scripting Jobs, Become A Freelancer Facebook, Best Sap Jobs, Beta Testing Jobs, Bi Analyst, Bi Freelance Jobs, Bi Freelance Projects, Big Data Finance Jobs, Big Data Hadoop Jobs, Bitcoin Freelance, Biztalk Freelance Projects, Blender 3d Freelance Jobs, Blockchain Developer Freelance, Blockchain Freelance Projects, Blockchain Jobs, Blogging Jobs, Bootstrap Freelance Jobs, Brighton Game Studios, BTC Freelancer, Build Website Freelance, Business Administration Work, Business Analyst Internship, Business Analyst Jobs, Business Analyst Telecommute, Business Consultant, Business Continuity Jobs, Business Data Analyst Jobs, Business Development Consultant Freelance, Business Development Executive Jobs, Business Improvement Manager, Business Improvement Specialist, Business Information Systems Jobs, Business Intelligence Graduate, Business Intelligence Jobs, Business Intelligence Manager, Business Objects Freelance Jobs, Business Systems Analyst, C Freelance Work, C Programming Jobs, C Software Engineer, C# Online Jobs, C# Programming Jobs, C++ Developer Jobs, C++ Finance Jobs, C++ Jobs, Cache Developer, Cad Design From Home, Cad Drawing Freelance, Cad Jobs, Cad Technician Jobs, CAE Freelance Jobs, Cakephp Freelancer, Catia Freelance Jobs, Catia V5 Jobs, CCIE Contract Jobs, CCNA, CCNA Indeed, CCNA Jobs With No Experience, CCNP Data Center Jobs, CGI Freelancer, Chief Engineer Jobs, Chief Information Officer Jobs, Chief Officer Jobs, Chief Operating Officer Jobs, CIO Jobs, CISO Jobs, CISSP Jobs, Clickfunnels Freelancer, Climate Technologies, Clojure Freelance Jobs, CNC Programming From Home, Cobol CICS Db2 Jobs, Cobol Jobs, Cobol Programming Jobs, CodeIgniter Freelance Jobs, Coding Freelance Work, ColdFusion Freelance Projects, ColdFusion Freelance Work, Comcast Jobs, Commercial Analyst Jobs, Companies Looking For New Logos, Companies Looking For Video Production, CompTIA A Plus Jobs, CompTIA Security Plus Jobs, Computational And Applied Mathematics Jobs,

Computer Assembly Jobs, Computer Coding Jobs, Computer Coding Jobs From Home, Computer Consultant, Computer Design Jobs, Computer Engineering Internships, Computer Engineering Jobs, Computer Forensics Jobs, Computer Forensics Technician, Computer Games Programming Jobs, Computer Jobs, Computer Jobs From Home, Computer Jobs With No Experience Needed, Computer Networking Jobs, Computer Operator Jobs, Computer Repair Jobs, Computer Science Graduate Jobs, Computer Science Internships, Computer Security Jobs, Computer Software Developer, Computer Support Jobs, Computer Support Specialist Jobs, Computer Technician Jobs, Computer Technology Certificate Jobs, Computer Trainer, Computer Vision Freelance Jobs, Consultant Sap Junior, Content Jobs, Content Writing Freelance Work, Content Writing Work From Home, Continuous Improvement Jobs, Contract Coding Companies, Contract It Jobs From Home, Contract Software Engineer, Control Systems Engineering, Control Systems Jobs, Copywriter Jobs, Copywriting Work, Core Java Developer Jobs, Core Java Freelance Jobs, Core Php Jobs, Corel Draw Jobs Online, CorelDRAW Work At Home, Corona SDK Freelancer, Corporate Governance Jobs, Creative Digital Marketing Jobs, Creo Freelance Jobs, CRM Business Analyst, CRM Jobs, CRM Manager Jobs, Crypto Custodian Jobs, Crystal Reports Freelance, CSIRO Jobs, CTO Contract Jobs, CTO Roles, Customer Logistics Analyst, Cyber Forensics Jobs, Cyber Intelligence, Cyber Security Apprenticeships, Cyber Security Consultant, Cyber Security Internships, Cyber Security Jobs, Cyber Security Police Jobs, Cyber Security Software Engineer, Cybernetics Jobs, D3 Js Freelance, Data Administrator, Data Analysis Jobs, Data Analyst Internship, Data Analyst Jobs, Data Analytics Consulting Jobs, Data Analytics Freelance Jobs, Data Center Jobs, Data Collection Freelancer, Data Curation Jobs, Data Encoder Online, Data Engineer Jobs, Data Entry Career, Data Entry Contract Jobs, Data Entry Jobs, Data Governance Jobs, Data Jobs, Data Jobs From Home, Data Migration Specialist, Data Mining, Data Mining Freelance, Data Privacy Jobs, Data Protection Jobs, Data Quality Analyst Jobs, Data Quality Jobs, Data Science Contract Jobs, Data Science Freelance, Data Science Jobs, Data Science Projects Freelance, Data Scientist Jobs, Data Solutions Architect, Data Strategy Jobs, Data Visualization Freelance, Data Visualization Jobs, Database Administrator Jobs, Database Analyst Jobs, Database Developer Jobs, Database Maintenance Job, Database Officer, Dba Contract Jobs, Dba Freelance Work, Dba Jobs, Deep Learning Freelance Jobs, Dell EMC, Delphi Freelance Work, Delphi Jobs, Design Engineer Jobs, Design Jobs, Design Student Jobs, Designer Photoshop Job, Deskside Support

Technician, Desktop Publishing Jobs, Desktop Support Analyst, Desktop Support Jobs, Developer Jobs, Developer Full Stack Freelance, DevOps Engineer Jobs, DevOps Freelance Jobs, DevOps Jobs, Digital Agency Jobs, Digital Analyst Jobs, Digital Analytics Analyst, Digital Architect Jobs, Digital Content Producer, Digital Copywriter Jobs, Digital Design, Digital Developer, Digital Director Jobs, Digital Forensics Jobs, Digital Intermediate Jobs, Digital Internships, Digital Jobs, Digital Manager Jobs, Digital Manufacturing Jobs, Digital Marketing Consultant, Digital Marketing Coordinator, Digital Marketing Director Jobs, Digital Marketing Freelance Projects, Digital Marketing Internship, Digital Marketing Jobs, Digital Marketing Manager Jobs, Digital Marketing Specialist, Digital Media Careers, Digital Product Manager, Digital Sales Jobs, Digital Strategy Manager, Digital Web Manager Job, Digital Work From Home Jobs, Director Of New Product Development, Distance Jobs, Django Freelance Projects, Dot Net Freelance Jobs, Dot Net Freelancer, Dream Jobs Work From Home, Dreamweaver Freelancer, Drone Freelance, Drone Pilot Jobs, Drupal Freelancer, Drupal Jobs, Drupal Web Developer Jobs, DTP Jobs Work From Home, DV Cleared Network Engineer, Dynamics 365 Freelancer, Dynamics AX Freelance Jobs, Dynamics CRM Freelance Jobs, Dynamics Nav Freelance Jobs, Ecommerce Freelance, Ecommerce Jobs, Editor Needed For YouTube, eLearning Developer, Email Marketing Freelancer, Email Marketing Jobs, Email Processing Jobs, Embedded Freelance, Embedded Jobs, Embedded Software Engineer Jobs, Embedded Systems, End User Services Manager Job Description, Entity Solutions, Entrepreneur Jobs, Entry Level Business Analyst Jobs, Entry Level Cisco Jobs, Entry Level Coding Jobs, Entry Level Computer Science Jobs, Entry Level Cyber Security Jobs, Entry Level Cyber Security Jobs No Experience, Entry Level Data Analyst Jobs, Entry Level Financial Analyst, Entry Level Help Desk, Entry Level It Jobs, Entry Level Programming Jobs, Entry Level Python Jobs, Entry Level Salesforce Jobs, Entry Level Software Engineer Jobs, Entry Level Technical Writer Jobs, Entry Level Work From Home Jobs, Epic Careers, ER Tech Jobs, ERP Consultant, ERP Freelance Jobs, Esports Jobs, Ethereum Freelance Jobs, ETL Freelance Jobs, Excel Freelance Jobs, Excel Jobs, Excel Jobs Online, Excel Macro Freelance, Excel Projects Online, Excel Spreadsheet Freelance Work, Excel VBA Jobs, Facebook Ads Manager Freelance, Facebook API Freelancer, Fibre Optic Jobs, Field Service Manager Jobs, Field Service Technician, Flash Animation Freelance Work, Flexible Jobs, Food Technology Jobs, Fortran Developer Jobs, Forum Posting Jobs, Freelance 2d Animation Jobs, Freelance 3d Architectural Visualization

Artist, Freelance 3d Modelling, Freelance 3d Printing Jobs, Freelance 3d Projects, Freelance Academic Writing Jobs Online, Freelance Access Programmer, Freelance Admin Jobs Online, Freelance Adobe Premiere Jobs, Freelance Advertising Design, Freelance AdWords Jobs, Freelance Amazon Web Services Jobs, Freelance Analyst Jobs, Freelance Android Application Developer, Freelance Android Developer, Freelance Angular, Freelance Angular 2 Developer, Freelance Animation Projects, Freelance App Design, Freelance Audio Editing Jobs, Freelance Audio Jobs, Freelance AutoCAD Jobs, Freelance AutoCAD Jobs From Home, Freelance Automation Projects, Freelance Automation Testing Jobs, Freelance Banner Design Jobs, Freelance Bi Jobs, Freelance Big Data Engineer, Freelance Blog Writer, Freelance Bloggers Wanted, Freelance Business Analyst, Freelance Business Development Jobs, Freelance C Programming Jobs, Freelance Cad Designer Jobs, Freelance Cad Work, Freelance Catia, Freelance Cloud Consultant, Freelance CNC Programming, Freelance CNC Work, Freelance Cobol Programming Jobs, Freelance Code Work, Freelance Coding Jobs, Freelance Coding Projects, Freelance Communications Jobs, Freelance Computer Engineer, Freelance Computer Jobs From Home, Freelance Computer Programming Jobs, Freelance Computer Security Work, Freelance Computer Support, Freelance Content Creator, Freelance Content Developer, Freelance Content Writing Jobs, Freelance Content Writing Projects, Freelance Copywriter Website, Freelance Copywriting Jobs, Freelance CSS Designer, Freelance Cyber Security Jobs, Freelance Data Analysis Jobs, Freelance Data Analytics Projects, Freelance Data Capturing, Freelance Data Collection Jobs, Freelance Data Entry, Freelance Data Jobs, Freelance Data Scientist, Freelance Data Scraping, Freelance Database Design, Freelance Database Developer Jobs, Freelance Database Jobs, Freelance Database Work, Freelance Dba Jobs, Freelance Dba Projects, Freelance Delphi, Freelance Development Consultant, Freelance Digital Marketing Services, Freelance Documentation, Freelance Dot Net Programmer, Freelance Dynamics CRM Consultant, Freelance Ecommerce Jobs, Freelance Ecommerce Manager, Freelance Editing Jobs, Freelance eLearning Jobs, Freelance Email Copywriter, Freelance Email Designer, Freelance Email Developer, Freelance Email Marketing Jobs, Freelance Embedded Programmer, Freelance Embedded Projects, Freelance Embedded Software Developer, Freelance Embedded Software Engineer, Freelance Excel Consultant, Freelance Excel Projects, Freelance Facebook Marketing, Freelance Flash Animation Jobs, Freelance Front End Developer Work, Freelance Front End Web Developer Jobs, Freelance

Fusion 360 Jobs, Freelance Game Designer, Freelance Game Jobs, Freelance GIS Digitizer, Freelance GIS Jobs Online, Freelance GIS Specialist, Freelance Graphic Artist Needed, Freelance Graphic Design Work, Freelance Graphic Designer, Freelance Graphic Jobs Online, Freelance Hadoop Developer, Freelance Help Desk Jobs, Freelance Help Desk Support, Freelance Home Based Data Entry Jobs, Freelance Html Coding Jobs, Freelance Html CSS Jobs, Freelance Html Designer, Freelance Html5 Game Developer, Freelance Industrial Design Work, Freelance Internet Researcher, Freelance iOS Developer, Freelance iPhone App Developer, Freelance It Jobs, Freelance It Projects, Freelance It Solutions, Freelance It Support Jobs, Freelance J2ee, Freelance Java J2ee Projects, Freelance Java Programming Jobs, Freelance Java Programming Work, Freelance Java Projects, Freelance JavaScript Jobs, Freelance JavaScript Work, Freelance Jobs 3d Max, Freelance Jobs, Freelance Jobs For Selenium Testing, Freelance Jobs For Selenium Testing, Freelance Jobs Html5, Freelance Jobs Machine Learning, Freelance Jobs Online, Freelance Jobs PowerPoint Presentation, Freelance Joomla Jobs, Freelance Linux, Freelance Linux Programmer, Freelance Machine Learning Engineer, Freelance Machine Learning Project, Freelance Market Research, Freelance Marketing Research Jobs, Freelance Media Production, Freelance Mobile App Testing, Freelance MS Access Jobs, Freelance MS Project, Freelance Net Developer, Freelance Network Technician, Freelance Newsletter Writer, Freelance Objective C, Freelance Operations Consultant, Freelance Oracle Consultant, Freelance Oracle Developer, Freelance Penetration Testing Jobs, Freelance Peoplesoft, Freelance Photo Editing Online, Freelance Photo Editor, Freelance Photoshop Jobs Online, Freelance Php Developer Jobs, Freelance Php MySQL Programmer, Freelance Pinterest, Freelance Pl SQL Developer, Freelance PMP, Freelance Podcast Editor Jobs, Freelance Ppt Presentation, Freelance Process Engineer, Freelance Product Designer, Freelance Product Developer, Freelance Product Development, Freelance Product Manager Jobs, Freelance Programming Jobs, Freelance Programming Projects, Freelance Project Manager Website, Freelance Proof Reader, Freelance Python Developer Jobs, Freelance QA Jobs, Freelance QA Tester, Freelance QA Testing Projects, Freelance R Programming, Freelance Raspberry Pi, Freelance React Developer, Freelance Rendering Jobs, Freelance Report Writing Jobs, Freelance Reporting Services, Freelance Research Projects, Freelance Robotics Engineer, Freelance Robotics Jobs, Freelance RPA, Freelance Ruby On Rails Developer, Freelance Ruby Programmer, Freelance SEO

Content Writing Jobs, Freelance SEO Jobs, Freelance ServiceNow Jobs, Freelance SharePoint Consultants, Freelance SharePoint Developer Jobs, Freelance Siemens Plc Programmer, Freelance Six Sigma Jobs, Freelance Social Media Content Creator, Freelance Social Media Designer, Freelance Social Media Jobs, Freelance Social Media Marketing Manager, Freelance Software Development Jobs, Freelance Software Jobs, Freelance Software Sales, Freelance Software Tester, Freelance Software Testing Trainer, Freelance Solidworks Jobs Online, Freelance Sound Jobs, Freelance SQL Programmer, Freelance SQL Server, Freelance SQL Server Developer, Freelance SSIS, Freelance Startup Jobs, Freelance Statistical Analysis, Freelance Swift Developer, Freelance Sysadmin Jobs, Freelance System Administrator Jobs, Freelance System Developer, Freelance Tableau, Freelance Tableau Consulting, Freelance Tech Work, Freelance Technical Support Jobs, Freelance Technical Writer Wanted, Freelance Telecom Jobs, Freelance Test Automation Projects, Freelance Testing Websites, Freelance Tutoring Websites, Freelance Unity Programmer, Freelance Usability Testing, Freelance VBA Developer, Freelance Video Editing Jobs, Freelance Video Editing Services, Freelance Video Game Designer, Freelance Video Maker, Freelance Videographer, Freelance Videoscribe, Freelance Virtual Assistant Jobs, Freelance Web App Developer, Freelance Web Application Projects, Freelance Web Content, Freelance Web Design Jobs, Freelance Web Design Jobs For Beginners, Freelance Web Design Work Online, Freelance Web Designer, Freelance Web Dev Jobs, Freelance Web Developer, Freelance Web Developer Jobs, Freelance Webmaster, Freelance WordPress, Freelance Writing Jobs Online, Freelance Zend, Freelancer API, Freelancer AutoCAD 2d, Freelancer Chatbot, Freelancer Content Marketing, Freelancer Customer Care, Freelancer Dedicated Server, Freelancer Mis Jobs, Freelancer MMO, Freelancer Mobile App Developer, Freelancer Twitter, Freelancer UX Design, Freelancer Wikipedia, Freelancing Jobs For Front End Developer, Freelancing Websites For Software Testing, Front End Developer, Front End Developer Internship, Front End Developer Remote Jobs, Front End Jobs, Front End Specialist, Front End Web Developer Jobs, Full Stack Developer, Full Stack Developer Remote, Fusion 360 Freelance, Game Design Jobs, Game Designer Jobs, Game Developer Jobs, Game Development Freelance Projects, Game Industry Jobs, Game Jobs, Game Programmer Jobs, Game Streaming Jobs, Game Studios, Game Tester Jobs, Game Tester Jobs At Home, Game Tester Jobs No Experience, Game Writer Jobs, GIS Analyst Jobs, GIS Freelance, GIS Jobs, GIS Specialist Jobs, Golang Freelance Jobs, Google Ad Jobs Online, Google Ads Freelancer,

Google AdSense Jobs, Google AdWords Freelancer, Google AdWords Work From Home, Google Analytics Freelance Jobs, Google Analytics Upwork, Google Australia, Google Jobs, Graduate Data Scientist Jobs, Graduate It Support Analyst, Graphic Artist Jobs, Graphic Design For Film Jobs, Graphic Design Gigs, Graphic Design Internship, Graphic Design Internships, Graphic Design Jobs, Graphic Design Work, Graphic Designer Herts, Graphic Designer Job, Graphic Work Online, Growth Hacker Freelance, Hadoop Administrator Jobs, Hadoop Freelance Jobs, Hardware Freelancer, Head Of It, Health Information Technology Jobs, Health Network Jobs, Healthcare Business Analyst, Help Desk Jobs, Helpdesk Support Jobs, HFC Technician Salary, Home Based Computer Jobs, Home Based Content Moderator, How To Get A Job In Internet Marketing, How To Get Freelance Animation Work, Hp Technical Support Jobs, Html Freelance Jobs, Html5 Freelance Jobs, Hull Graphic Design Jobs, Hyperion Jobs, Hyperion Planning Jobs, IBM Help Desk Jobs, IBM Jobs, IBM ODM Developer, IBM Part Time, IBM Solution Architect, ICT Apprenticeships, ICT Architect, ICT Manager Jobs, ICT Police Jobs, Illustrator Jobs, Indeed Computer Science Internship, Indeed Sap Basis Jobs, InDesign Freelancer, InDesign Work From Home, Indie Game Audio Jobs, Industrial Automation Freelance Job, Info Technology Jobs, Infographic Freelance Jobs, Infojobs, Informatica Contract Jobs, Informatica Freelance Jobs, Informatica Freelancing Projects, Information Analyst, Information And Knowledge Management Jobs, Information And Technology Jobs, Information Literacy Librarian, Information Manager, Information Officer, Information Resource Management Jobs, Information Security Freelance, Information Security Jobs, Information Systems Business Analyst, Information Technology Developer, Information Technology Jobs, Information Technology Management Jobs, Infosys Australia Jobs, Innovation Development Manager, Instagram Consultant Jobs, Instagram Content Creator Job, Instagram Jobs, Integration Specialist, Intelligence Analyst Jobs, Intelligence Gathering Jobs, Interface Jobs, Internal Quality Assurance Jobs, International Ad Posting Jobs, International Online Jobs For Encoder, Internet Based Jobs From Home, Internet Freelancer, Internet Marketing Jobs, Internet Research Jobs From Home, Intuit Business Data Analyst, Inventor Freelance Jobs, Ionic Framework Jobs, Ionic Freelancer, iOS Developer, iOS Freelance Jobs, IoT Consulting Jobs, iPad Jobs, iPhone Developer Melbourne, iPhone Freelance Projects, It Administrator Jobs, It Apprenticeships, It Asset Management Analyst Job Description, It Assistant, It Audit Jobs, It Auditor Jobs, It Business Analyst, It Business

Development, It Business Support Analyst, It Consultant Jobs, It Contractor, It Contracts, It Delivery Manager, It Developer, It Development Program, It Director Jobs, It Graduate Schemes, It Help Desk Jobs, It Infrastructure Jobs, It Internship, It Job, It Jobs With No Experience Required, It Manager Jobs, It Networking Internship, It Officer, It Onsite Support, It Program Manager, It Project Jobs, It Project Manager Jobs, It Sales Jobs, It Security Consultant, It Security Jobs, It Service Delivery, It Service Delivery Manager, It Site Manager, It Software Development Jobs, It Specialist, It Support, It Support Analyst Jobs, It Support Jobs, It Support Technician Jobs, It Systems Administrator Jobs, It Systems Engineer, It Teaching Jobs, It Tech Jobs, It Technician Jobs, It Trainee, It Traineeships, It Trainer Jobs, It Vendor Manager, It Worker, It Works Jobs, Java Business Analyst, Java Developer Jobs, Java Developer Positions, Java Freelance Jobs Online, Java Graduate Jobs, Java Jobs, Java Outsourcing Jobs, Java Spring Jobs, JavaFX Freelancer, JavaScript Developer Jobs, JavaScript Freelance Projects, JavaScript Jobs, JavaScript Online Jobs, JDE Technical, Job Typing Books Into eBooks, Jobs Based On Ms Office, Jobs Biotech, Jobs C, Jobs For Coders Online, Jobs For Computer Science Students, Jobs Working From Home On Computer, Joomla Freelance Jobs, Joomla Programmers For Hire, Junior Analyst, Junior Analyst Jobs, Junior Business Intelligence, Junior Developer, Junior Front End Developer, Junior Game Developer Jobs, Junior Graphic Design Jobs, Junior It Jobs, Junior Java Developer Freelance, Junior Java Developer Jobs, Junior JavaScript Developer Jobs, Junior Network Engineer, Junior Online, Junior Oracle Dba Jobs, Junior Programmer Jobs, Junior Python Developer Freelance, Junior Sap Jobs, Junior Software Developer, Junior Software Tester, Junior SQL Jobs, Junior Test Analyst Jobs, Junior Tester Jobs, Junior User Experience Jobs, Junior Web Designer, Junior Web Developer Jobs, Keyword Research Freelance Jobs, LabVIEW Freelance Projects, Laravel Freelance Jobs, Latex Freelance, Lead Business Systems Analyst Job, Lean Six Sigma Jobs, Learning And Development Jobs, Library It Jobs, Lidar Jobs Online, Liferay Freelance Jobs, Lims Administrator, Link Building Jobs Online, Link Posting Jobs, Linux Admin Jobs, Linux Engineer Jobs, Linux Jobs, Linux System Administrator Freelance Jobs, Logo Design Work, Looking For Digital Artist, Looking For Email Marketing, Looking For Videographer, Mac It Jobs, Mac Jobs Leeds, Machine Learning Jobs, Machine Learning Online Jobs, Magento Developer Freelance, Magento Developer, Magento Jobs, Magento Projects Freelance, Magento Work, Mailchimp Freelancer, Mainframe Freelance Projects, Mainframe Jobs, Managing Instagram

Accounts Job, Market Research Analyst Jobs, Market Research Projects Online, Market Researchers, Marketing Automation Jobs, Marketing Jobs, Marketing Web Developer Job, Master Data Jobs, MATLAB Freelance Work, MATLAB Online Jobs, MATLAB Programming Jobs Online, Maven Freelance, Maya Rigging Freelance Work, Media Communications Jobs, Media Internships, Media Jobs, Medical Coding Jobs, Metrics Reporting Analyst Job, Microsoft Access Administration, Microsoft Access Programming Jobs, Microsoft CRM Jobs, Microsoft Dynamics AX Freelance, Microsoft Dynamics CRM Consultant, Microsoft Dynamics CRM Developer, Microsoft Excel Consulting Jobs, Microsoft Office Jobs, Microsoft Office Jobs From Home, Microsoft Word Jobs, MicroStation Freelancer, Midi Programmer, Mis Jobs, Mobile App Testing Jobs From Home, Mobile Developer Jobs, MS Access Jobs Remote, MS Access Programming Jobs, MS Excel Online Jobs, MS Jobs, MS Office Jobs Online, MS Word Jobs, Music Software Developer, MySQL Database Developer, MySQL Freelance Jobs, Nasa Cyber Security Internship, Nav Freelancer, NBN Installer Jobs, Net Developer, Net Jobs, NetSuite Freelance Jobs, Network Administrator Jobs, Network Analysis Freelance, Network Analyst, Network Engineer, Network Engineer Jobs, Network Security Jobs, Network Support Technician, Networking Jobs, Ngo It Jobs, NHS It Contract, NOC Engineer, Node Js Developer Freelance, Node Js Freelance Projects, Odoo Freelance Jobs, Odoo Upwork, Offsite Graphic Designer Wanted, Oil And Gas It Jobs, Online Academic Research Writing Jobs, Online Affiliate Marketing Jobs, Online Assistant, Online Audio Engineering Jobs, Online Automation Testing Jobs, Online Bookkeeping Jobs, Online BPO, Online Cad Drafting Jobs, Online Cad Work, Online Coding Jobs In Java, Online Crypto Jobs, Online Customer Service Jobs, Online Data Editing Jobs, Online Data Entry Jobs, Online Data Entry Work, Online Documentation Jobs, Online ESL Jobs, Online Excel Work Job, Online Freelance Marketing, Online Game Design Jobs, Online Game Development Jobs, Online Game Review Jobs, Online Game Tester Job Openings, Online Graphic Design Jobs, Online Instructor Jobs, Online Internships, Online Internships For College Students, Online It Projects Jobs, Online Jobs, Online Jobs For Biotechnology Students, Online Jobs From Home, Online Jobs Hiring, Online Jobs In Digital Marketing, Online Machine Learning Jobs, Online Marketing Internships, Online Marketing Research Jobs, Online Outsourcing Work, Online Paid Jobs, Online Part Time Jobs From Home, Online Photo Editing Jobs, Online Photoshop Jobs, Online Php Project Work, Online Programming Jobs, Online Project Work In Html, Online Projects On Python, Online SEO Projects Jobs, Online SEO

Work Projects, Online Social Media Jobs, Online Software Projects For Developers, Online System Admin Jobs, Online Teaching Jobs Australia, Online Tech Support Jobs Work From Home, Online Tutoring Australia, Online Tutoring Jobs, Online Video Editing Jobs, Online Web Hosting Jobs, Online Work From Home, OpenCart Expert Freelancer, Operations Manager Jobs, Operations Manager Jobs Aberdeen, Optical Network Engineer Job Description, Oracle Apps Freelance Work, Oracle Apps Jobs, Oracle Bpm Jobs, Oracle Database Administrator, Oracle Database Engineer, Oracle Dba Contract, Oracle Dba Jobs, Oracle EBS Freelance Jobs, Oscommerce Freelancer, Outsource Projects Jobs, Paid Graphic Design Internships, Part Time 3d Renderer, Part Time Data Science Jobs, Part Time It Jobs, Part Time Pc Repair Jobs, Part Time Virtual Assistant Jobs, Part Time Virtual Jobs, Pay Per Click Jobs From Home, PayPal Freelancer, Pc Hardware Technician Jobs, Pdf Conversion Jobs Home, Pdf Conversion Jobs Online, Pega Developer Jobs, Peoplesoft Jobs, Performance Analyst, Performance Management Consultant Job Description, Phalcon Php Jobs, PhoneGap Freelancer, PhoneGap Jobs, Photo Editing Jobs, Photoshop Design Work, Photoshop Designer Jobs Online, Photoshop Editing Work At Home, Php Developer Jobs, Php Freelancer Needed, Php Jobs, Php Online Jobs, Pinterest Freelance Jobs, Pl SQL Freelance Projects, Placement Websites, Planning Freelance, Plc Programmer Freelance Work, Podcast Editing Jobs, Podcast Jobs, Podcast Producer, Pos Designer Jobs, Power Bi Freelance Jobs, PowerPoint Freelance, PowerPoint Jobs From Home, PowerPoint Jobs Online, PowerShell Freelance, PPC Expert Jobs, Pre Sales Engineer, Presentation Designer Jobs, Presentation Freelance, Prezi Freelancer, Principal Business Systems Analyst Job, Process Analyst, Process Engineer Jobs, Product Developer Jobs, Product Development Jobs, Product Engineer, Professional Jobs, Programming Jobs, Programming Side Jobs, Project Analyst Jobs, Project Engineer Jobs, Project Officer Jobs, Project Writing Jobs Online, Promoter Jobs Instagram, PSD To Html Remote Jobs, Publishing Design Jobs, Python Developer Freelance Jobs, Python Developer Jobs, Python Django Developer, Python Jobs, Python Online Jobs, Python Programming Jobs, QA Analyst Jobs, QA Game Tester Jobs, QA Officer, QlikView Freelance Projects, Quality Analyst, Quality Control Manager, Quality Manager Jobs, Quantitative Analyst, R Programming Freelance Jobs, R Programming Jobs, R&D Project Manager, Raspberry Pi Freelancer, React Developer, React Developer Freelance, React Js Freelance Work, React Native Upwork, Real Telecommute Jobs, Remote Analyst Jobs, Remote Business Analyst Jobs, Remote Cad Jobs, Remote

Copy Editor Jobs, Remote Cyber Security Jobs, Remote Data Analyst Jobs, Remote Data Entry, Remote Data Science Jobs, Remote Developer Jobs, Remote Graphic Design Jobs, Remote Help Desk Support, Remote Internships, Remote It Jobs, Remote Jobs Online, Remote Programming Jobs, Remote Research Jobs, Remote Social Media Jobs, Remote Software Engineer Jobs, Remote Technical Writer, Remote UI UX Jobs, Remote Video Editing Jobs, Remote Web Developer Jobs, Remote WordPress Jobs, Remote Work From Home Jobs, Repair And Fix Computer Jobs, Research Analyst Jobs, Research Analyst, Research Assistant Jobs, Research Jobs, Responsive Web Design Jobs, Ruby Jobs, Ruby On Rails Freelance Projects, Ruby Programming Jobs, SaaS Sales Career, Salesforce Admin Freelance Jobs, Salesforce Admin Jobs, Salesforce Administrator Jobs, Salesforce Consultant, Salesforce Database Administrator, Salesforce Developer Jobs, Salesforce Entry Level Jobs, Salesforce Freelance, Salesforce Freelance Trainer, Salesforce Jobs Leeds, Salesforce Projects Online, Sap ABAP Freelance Jobs, Sap ABAP Freelance Projects, Sap ABAP Jobs, Sap ABAP Online Jobs, Sap ABAP Projects Online, Sap Apo Jobs, Sap Bi Analyst, Sap Bi Freelance Jobs, Sap BPC Freelance, Sap Business Analyst Jobs, Sap Business Analyst Jobs, Sap CRM Jobs, Sap Data Migration Jobs, Sap Fico Contract Jobs, Sap Freelance Jobs, Sap Freelancing Projects, Sap Functional Consultant Jobs, Sap Hana Freelance Projects, Sap Hybris Jobs, Sap Jobs, Sap Online Jobs, Sap Planner Jobs, Sap Procurement Jobs, Sap Security Freelance Jobs, Sap Security Jobs, Sap Specialist, SAS Freelance Jobs, SAS Jobs, SAS Programmer, Satellite Technician, Scada Engineer, Scada Network Engineer, Scala And Big Data, Scientific Computing Jobs, Scope Of Computer Science In Australia, Scraping Work, Scrum Master Jobs, SDN Developer, Search Engine Optimization Freelance Jobs, Security Manager Jobs, Security Operations Manager Jobs, Siemens, Select Solutions Jobs, Selenium Freelance Jobs, Senior Business Development Manager Jobs, Senior Data Analyst, Senior Designer, Senior Digital Marketing Manager, Senior Field Technician, Senior Information Security Consultant, Senior Integration Engineer Job Description, Senior NOC Engineer Job Description, Senior Social Media Manager Job Description, Senior Tableau Developer, SEO Analyst Freelance, SEO Freelance Work From Home, SEO Freelancer, SEO Jobs, SEO Manager, SEO Marketing Jobs, SEO Specialist, SEO Writing Jobs, SEO Writing Jobs Online, Service Desk Jobs, Service Level Manager Jobs, Service Technician Jobs, Service Virtualization Jobs, ServiceNow Freelance Work, ServiceNow Jobs, ServiceNow Online Jobs, SharePoint Jobs, SharePoint Solution Architect,

SharePoint Specialist, Shopify Freelancer, Siemens Rugby, Simple Programming Jobs, Site Admin Jobs, Six Sigma Black Belt Jobs, Sketchup Freelancer, Sketchup Jobs, Social Marketing Jobs, Social Media Consultant Jobs, Social Media Content Creator, Social Media Content Evaluator, Social Media Content Moderator, Social Media Intern, Social Media Jobs, Social Media Management Freelance Jobs, Social Media Manager Jobs, Social Media Marketing Freelance, Social Media Marketing Needed, Software Deployment Engineer Job, Software Developer Apprenticeship, Software Developer Internship, Software Developer Jobs, Software Development Gigs, Software Development Internship, Software Development Jobs, Software Development Manager, Software Development Projects Freelance, Software Development Work, Software Engineer Internship, Software Engineer Jobs, Software Engineer Summer Intern, Software Engineer Travel Jobs, Software Engineering Jobs, Software Engineering Manager, Software Intern, Software Jobs, Software Programmer, Software Project Leader, Software Research Jobs, Software Sales Jobs, Software Technology Jobs, Software Test Engineer, Software Testing Contract Jobs, Software Testing Jobs, Software Testing Projects For Freelancers, Solidworks 3d Modelling Jobs, Solidworks Contract Work, Solidworks Drafting Jobs From Home, Solidworks Jobs, Solution Architect Contract Jobs, Solution Architect Jobs, Solutions Engineer, Sound Design Work, Spark Freelancers, Splunk Freelance Jobs, SQL, SQL Data Analyst, SQL Database Developer, SQL Developer Jobs, Squarespace Consultant, Squarespace Freelance, SSIS Freelance Jobs, Starter It Jobs, Startup Consulting Jobs, Strategic Planning Careers, Strategy And Business Development Analyst, Strategy Manager, Support Tech, Swift Freelance Jobs, Symfony Freelance Jobs, Sysadmin Jobs, System Administrator Jobs, System Support Technician Job, Systems Analyst Jobs, Tableau Jobs, Tableau Online Jobs, Tech Design Jobs, Tech Internships, Tech Jobs With No Experience, Tech Support Jobs From Home, Tech Support Jobs, Tech Writers Wanted, Techforce, Technical Architect, Technical Author Jobs, Technical Business Analyst Jobs, Technical Document Controller, Technical Marketing Consultant, Technical Support Freelance Jobs, Technical Support Jobs, Technical Support Specialist, Technical Writer Jobs, Technology Assistant Jobs, Technology Sales Consultant, Telecom Consulting Jobs, Telecom Engineer, Telecom Project Engineer, Telecom Strategy Jobs, Telecommunications Jobs, Telecommunications Technician, Telecommute Customer Service Jobs, Telecommuting Jobs, Telecommuting Technology Jobs, Telework Jobs, Telstra Jobs, Telstra

Media, Test Analyst Jobs, Test Architect Jobs, Test Design Engineer, Test Manager, Testing Freelance Projects, Trainee It Technician, Trainee Project Manager Jobs, Training And Development Jobs, Transaction Analyst, Travel Agent Jobs From Home, Types Of Database Jobs, UAT Jobs, UAV Jobs, Ui Design Freelance Work, Ui Design Internship, Ui Designer Jobs, UI UX Designer Freelance, UI UX Designer Jobs, Umbraco Freelancer, Unity 3d Freelance Work, Unity Contract Work, Unity Jobs, Unity Software Engineer, University It Jobs, University Research Assistant Jobs, Unreal Engine Freelance Jobs, Upwork Android Test, Upwork Aws, Upwork Banner, Upwork C, Upwork Chatbot, Upwork Customer Service Jobs, Upwork Database, Upwork Deep Learning, Upwork Digital Marketing, Upwork Django Developer, Upwork Editing Jobs, Upwork Excel, Upwork Front End Developer, Upwork Full Stack Developer, Upwork Google, Upwork Java Developer, Upwork JavaScript, Upwork Payment Gateway, Upwork R Programming, Upwork Salesforce Jobs, Upwork Social Media Marketing, Upwork Software, Upwork Unity Developer, Upwork Web Design, Upwork Wiki, Upwork WooCommerce, UX Design Internship, UX Design, UX Designer Jobs, UX Internship, UX Jobs, UX Specialist Jobs, UX Writer Jobs, VB Net Online Jobs, VBA Freelance Work, VBA Work, VFX Internship, VFX Work From Home, Video Animation Jobs, Video Editing Projects Online, Video Editing Work, Video Editor Jobs, Video Game Designer Jobs, Video Game Internships, Video Game Streaming Jobs, Video Game Tester From Home, Video Game Tester Jobs, Video Game Writer Jobs, Videographer Jobs, Virtual Administrative Assistant, Virtual Administrative Consultant, Virtual Assistant Jobs, Virtual Assistant Jobs For Beginners, Virtual Assistant Jobs, Virtual Assistant Jobs Work From Home, Virtual Customer Service Jobs, Virtual Data Entry Jobs, Virtual Jobs, Virtual Jobs From Home, Virtual Jobs Online, Virtual Support, Virtual Teaching Jobs, Virtual Technical Writer, Virtual Worlds Jobs, Virtual Writing Jobs, Visual Basic 6.0 Work Online, Visual Basic Freelance Work, Visual Effects Jobs, VP It Jobs, VR Internship, Vue Js Jobs, Vuejs Freelance, Web Analyst, Web Application Development Freelance, Web Application Development Jobs, Web Content Writing Projects, Web Design Jobs, Web Design Jobs Online, Web Design Online Work, Web Design Online Work, Web Design Projects Freelance, Web Design Work, Web Designer Freelance Website, Web Designer Freelancer, Web Designer Job, Web Developer, Web Developer Graphic Designer, Web Developer Internship, Web Developer Jobs, Web Producer, Web Research Companies, Web Research Jobs, Web Scraping Jobs Online, Webgl Freelance, Website Content Moderator Jobs, Website

Creator Job, Website Developer Jobs Online, Webstore Com Jobs, Wiki Upwork, Wireless System Engineer, Wireless Technician, Wix Designer Jobs, Wix Developer Jobs, WooCommerce Freelancer, WordPress Freelance Jobs, WordPress Freelance Jobs Plugin, Work As A Graphic Designer Online, Work From Home Customer Service Jobs, Work From Home Flexible Hours, Work From Home Job Postings, Work From Home Jobs, Work From Home Jobs Data Entry, Work From Home Software Testing Jobs, Work In Net, Work Remotely Jobs, Working At Microsoft Store, Working From Home, Xbox Jobs, Xml Freelance Jobs, Yahoo Jobs, YouTube Freelancer, YouTube Jobs Online, YouTube Subtitle Job, YouTube Video Editor Jobs, Zapier Freelancer, ZOHO CRM Jobs, ZOHO Developer Jobs, ZOHO Freelancer, Zoom Freelance

Now that you have your suitable IT Roles shortlist, use the list to match up IT Roles from the 6 job websites in the following chapters.

6 TOP 250+ ROLES IN IT ON SEEK WITH SALARIES (AUSTRALIA)

Compare your IT Role shortlist with those found on Seek. Note the minimum and maximum salaries if there is a match. Salaries are in Australian dollars. $1 AUD = $0.68 US = £0.53 UK. Click on the links to find all the vacancies under IT Roles of interest. The digital tool for this chapter is https://itjobsformula.com/seek/

Seek Job Title	Salary Min	Salary Max	URL Link
Agile Business Analyst	$80,000	$150,000	
https://www.seek.com.au/career-guide/role/agile-business-analyst			
Analyst jobs	$55,000	$120,000	
https://www.seek.com.au/analyst-jobs			
Android Developer	$50,000	$130,000	
https://www.seek.com.au/android-developer-jobs			
Angular 2 Developer	$120,000		
https://www.seek.com.au/angular-2-jobs			
Animation jobs	$75,000	$118,000	
https://www.seek.com.au/animation-jobs			
ASP Net Developer	$65,000	$120,000	
https://www.seek.com.au/net-developer-jobs			

Assistant Development Manager $45,000 $140,000
https://www.seek.com.au/assistant-development-manager-jobs/in-Brisbane-QLD-4000

Associate Business Analyst $65,000 $106,000
https://www.seek.com.au/associate-business-analyst-jobs

BI Analyst $100,000 $140,000
https://www.seek.com.au/business-intelligence-analyst-jobs

Business Administration work $74,000 $130,000
https://www.seek.com.au/business-administration-jobs

Business Analyst jobs $80,000 $110,000
https://www.seek.com.au/business-analyst-jobs

Business Improvement Analyst $87,000 $120,000
https://www.seek.com.au/business-improvement-analyst-jobs

Business Improvement Manager $110,000 $120,000
https://www.seek.com.au/business-improvement-manager-jobs

Business Improvement Specialist $90,000 $102,000
https://www.seek.com.au/business-improvement-jobs

Business Information Systems jobs $69,000 $96,000
https://www.seek.com.au/information-systems-jobs

Business Intelligence Graduate $55,000
https://www.seek.com.au/graduate-business-intelligence-jobs

Business Intelligence jobs $80,000 $180,000
https://www.seek.com.au/business-intelligence-jobs/in-All-Sydney-NSW

Business Intelligence Manager $90,000 $160,000
https://www.seek.com.au/business-intelligence-manager-jobs

C programmer jobs $120,000 $150,000

https://www.seek.com.au/c-programmer-jobs

C Software Engineer $90,000 $200,000
https://www.seek.com.au/c-software-engineer-jobs

Chief Engineer jobs $97,000 $220,000
https://www.seek.com.au/chief-engineer-jobs

Chief Officer jobs $140,000 $150,000
https://www.seek.com.au/chief-officer-jobs

CIO jobs $140,000 $200,000
https://www.seek.com.au/chief-information-officer-jobs

Cobol jobs $90,000 $120,000
https://www.seek.com.au/cobol-jobs

Commercial Analyst $70,000 $125,000
https://www.seek.com.au/commercial-analyst-jobs

Communications Coordinator $25,000 $111,000
https://www.seek.com.au/communications-coordinator-jobs

Computer Assembly jobs $45,000 $60,000
https://www.seek.com.au/computer-assembly-jobs

Computer Design jobs $70,000 $120,000
https://www.seek.com.au/jobs-in-design-architecture/graphic-design

Computer Engineering jobs $55,000 $65,000
https://www.seek.com.au/computer-engineer-jobs

Computer Forensics jobs $65,000 $120,000
https://www.seek.com.au/computer-forensics-jobs

Computer Games Programming jobs $90,000 $100,000
https://www.seek.com.au/game-programmer-jobs

Computer Networking jobs $45,000 $120,000

https://www.seek.com.au/networking-jobs

Computer Operator job $40,000 $45,000
https://www.seek.com.au/computer-operator-jobs

Computer Security jobs $65,000 $85,000
https://www.seek.com.au/cyber-security-jobs

Computer Software Developer $60,000 $120,000
https://www.seek.com.au/software-developer-jobs

Computer Technician jobs $40,000 $55,000
https://www.seek.com.au/computer-technician-jobs

Continuous Improvement Roles $120,000
https://www.seek.com.au/continuous-improvement-jobs

Contract Coding $87,000 $95,000
https://www.seek.com.au/coding-jobs/contract-temp

Contract IT Jobs from Home $60,000 $70,000
https://www.seek.com.au/work-from-home-jobs/contract-temp

Contract Software Engineer
https://www.seek.com.au/software-engineer-jobs/contract-temp

Control System jobs $65,000 $120,000
https://www.seek.com.au/control-systems-engineer-jobs

Core Java Developer jobs $85,000 $140,000
https://www.seek.com.au/core-java-jobs

Corporate Governance jobs $110,000 $120,000
https://www.seek.com.au/corporate-governance-jobs

CRM Business Analyst $120,000 $140,000
https://www.seek.com.au/crm-business-analyst-jobs

CRM jobs $70,000 $160,000
https://www.seek.com.au/crm-jobs/in-All-Sydney-NSW

CRM Manager $80,000 $130,000
https://www.seek.com.au/crm-manager-jobs

Cyber Forensics jobs $55,000 $130,000
https://www.seek.com.au/computer-forensics-jobs

Cyber Security jobs $100,000 $180,000
https://www.seek.com.au/cyber-security-jobs

Data Administrator $55,000 $70,000
https://www.seek.com.au/database-administrator-jobs

Data Analyst jobs $55,000 $90,000
https://www.seek.com.au/data-analyst-jobs

Data Analytics Consulting jobs $90,000 $180,000
https://www.seek.com.au/data-consultant-jobs

Data Centre jobs $70,000 $95,000
https://www.seek.com.au/data-center-jobs

Data Curation jobs $60,000 $132,000
https://www.seek.com.au/data-curation-jobs

Data Entry career $45,000 $80,000
https://www.seek.com.au/data-entry-jobs

Data Entry Contract jobs $30,000 $70,000
https://www.seek.com.au/data-entry-jobs/contract-temp

Data jobs $60,000 $130,000
https://www.seek.com.au/data-jobs

Data Jobs from Home $60,000 $140,000
https://www.seek.com.au/work-from-home-data-entry-jobs

Data Migration Specialist $150,000 $180,000
https://www.seek.com.au/data-migration-jobs

Data Mining $100,000 $160,000
https://www.seek.com.au/data-mining-jobs

Data Privacy jobs $82,000 $190,000
https://www.seek.com.au/data-protection-jobs

Data Quality jobs $75,000 $150,000
https://www.seek.com.au/data-quality-jobs

Data Visualization jobs $70,000 $170,000
https://www.seek.com.au/data-visualisation-jobs

Database Administrator jobs $75,000 $90,000
https://www.seek.com.au/database-administrator-jobs

Database Analyst jobs $97,000 $116,000
https://www.seek.com.au/data-analyst-jobs

Database Developer jobs $50,000 $100,000
https://www.seek.com.au/database-developer-jobs

Database Officer $82,000 $89,000
https://www.seek.com.au/database-officer-jobs

Design Engineer jobs$60,000 $140,000
https://www.seek.com.au/design-engineer-jobs

Desktop Support Analyst $55,000 $85,000
https://www.seek.com.au/desktop-support-analyst-jobs

Development Manager jobs $60,000 $200,000
https://www.seek.com.au/senior-development-manager-jobs

Digital Architect jobs$120,000 $140,000
https://www.seek.com.au/digital-architect-jobs

Digital Content Producer $77,000 $120,000
https://www.seek.com.au/digital-content-producer-jobs/in-Melbourne-VIC-3000

Digital Design $70,000 $90,000
https://www.seek.com.au/digital-designer-jobs

Digital Forensics jobs $110,000 $120,000
https://www.seek.com.au/Digital-Forensics-jobs

Digital Marketing Coordinator $50,000 $80,000
https://www.seek.com.au/digital-marketing-coordinator-jobs

Digital Marketing Specialist $85,000 $125,000
https://www.seek.com.au/digital-marketing-specialist-jobs

Digital Media careers $50,000 $130,000
https://www.seek.com.au/digital-media-jobs

Digital Product Manager $80,000 $140,000
https://www.seek.com.au/digital-product-manager-jobs

Drupal Web Developer jobs $75,000 $140,000
https://www.seek.com.au/drupal-jobs

Ecommerce jobs $40,000 $200,000
https://www.seek.com.au/ecommerce-jobs/in-All-Sydney-NSW

Elearning Developer $80,000 $120,000
https://www.seek.com.au/elearning-developer-jobs

Embedded Systems $80,000 $140,000
https://www.seek.com.au/embedded-system-jobs

Entrepreneur jobs $65,000 $120,000
https://www.seek.com.au/entrepreneur-jobs

Entry Level Business Analyst $55,000 $75,000
https://www.seek.com.au/business-analyst-entry-level-jobs

Entry Level Cisco jobs $55,000 $70,000
https://www.seek.com.au/entry-level-network-engineer-jobs

Entry Level Computer Science jobs $40,000 $55,000 https://www.seek.com.au/computer-science-graduate-jobs

Entry Level IT jobs $45,000 $80,000
https://www.seek.com.au/entry-level-jobs/in-All-Melbourne-VIC

Entry Level Software Engineer jobs $85,000
https://www.seek.com.au/entry-level-developer-jobs

ERP Consultant $70,000 $140,000
https://www.seek.com.au/erp-consultant-jobs

ETL Developer jobs $95,000 $110,000
https://www.seek.com.au/etl-developer-jobs

Field Service Manager $65,000
https://www.seek.com.au/field-service-manager-jobs

Field Service Technician $55,000 $75,000
https://www.seek.com.au/field-service-technician-jobs

Food Technology Government jobs $50,000 $70,000
https://www.seek.com.au/jobs-in-science-technology/food-technology-safety

Freelance Graphics Designer $55,000 $65,000
https://www.seek.com.au/freelance-graphic-designer-jobs/in-All-Melbourne-VIC

Game Industry jobs $65,000 $80,000
https://www.seek.com.au/video-games-jobs

Game Programmer jobs $90,000 $140,000
https://www.seek.com.au/game-programmer-jobs

Google jobs $50,000 $120,000
https://www.seek.com.au/Google-jobs/in-All-Brisbane-QLD

Graphic Design jobs $45,000 $80,000
https://www.seek.com.au/graphic-designer-jobs

Head of IT $110,000 $200,000
https://www.seek.com.au/head-of-it-jobs

Health Informatics jobs $75,000 $126,000
https://www.seek.com.au/health-informatics-jobs

Health Information jobs $50,000 $76,000
https://www.seek.com.au/health-information-jobs

Health IT jobs $70,000 $160,000
https://www.seek.com.au/health-it-jobs

Health Network jobs $67,000 $150,000
https://www.seek.com.au/primary-health-network-jobs

Home Based Computer jobs
https://www.seek.com.au/work-from-home-jobs

HP Technical Support jobs $80,000 $84,000
https://www.seek.com.au/Hewlett-Packard-jobs

Hyperion jobs $100,000 $150,000
https://www.seek.com.au/hyperion-jobs

ICT Manager jobs $140,000 $200,000
https://www.seek.com.au/ict-manager-jobs

Info Technology jobs $100,000 $122,000
https://www.seek.com.au/information-technology-jobs

Information Analyst $69,000 $150,000
https://www.seek.com.au/information-analyst-jobs

Information and Knowledge Management jobs $65,000
      $110,000
https://www.seek.com.au/knowledge-management-jobs

Information and Technology jobs $80,000 $85,000
https://www.seek.com.au/information-technology-jobs

Information Manager $90,000 $140,000
https://www.seek.com.au/information-manager-jobs

Information Officer jobs $60,000 $96,000
https://www.seek.com.au/information-officer-jobs

Information Resource Management jobs $60,000 $111,000
https://www.seek.com.au/resource-management-jobs

Information Systems Business Analyst $69,000 $77,000
https://www.seek.com.au/career-guide/role/information-technology-business-analyst

Information Technology jobs $55,000 $73,000
https://www.seek.com.au/jobs-in-information-communication-technology/in-All-Melbourne-VIC

Information Technology Management jobs $69,000 $160,000
https://www.seek.com.au/technology-management-jobs

Infosys jobs $55,000 $110,000
https://www.seek.com.au/Infosys-jobs

Integration Specialist $150,000 $170,000
https://www.seek.com.au/integration-specialist-jobs

Intelligence Analyst jobs $65,000 $97,000
https://www.seek.com.au/intelligence-analyst-jobs

Interface jobs $96,000 $108,000
https://www.seek.com.au/Interface-jobs

Internet Marketing jobs $50,000 $65,000
https://www.seek.com.au/online-marketing-jobs

IOS Developer $110,000 $130,000
https://www.seek.com.au/ios-developer-jobs/in-All-Melbourne-VIC

IoT Consulting jobs $95,000 $180,000
https://www.seek.com.au/iot-jobs

IT Assistant $65,000 $80,000
https://www.seek.com.au/it-assistant-jobs

IT Business Analyst $90,000 $135,000
https://www.seek.com.au/it-business-analyst-jobs

IT Business Development $50,000 $200,000
https://www.seek.com.au/business-development-jobs

IT Business Support Analyst $90,000 $110,000
https://www.seek.com.au/business-support-analyst-jobs

IT Consultant jobs $110,000 $150,000
https://www.seek.com.au/it-consultant-jobs

IT Delivery Manager $125,000 $150,000
https://www.seek.com.au/delivery-manager-jobs

IT Developer$90,000 $120,000
https://www.seek.com.au/software-developer-jobs

IT Help Desk jobs $40,000 $66,000
https://www.seek.com.au/jobs-in-information-communication-technology/help-desk-it-support/in-All-Melbourne-VIC

IT Jobs from Home $100,000 $140,000
https://www.seek.com.au/work-from-home-jobs/contract-temp

IT Jobs in Banks $80,000 $125,000
https://www.seek.com.au/bank-jobs

IT Jobs with No Experience $50,000 $55,000
https://www.seek.com.au/no-experience-jobs

IT Manager jobs $140,000 $180,000
https://www.seek.com.au/it-manager-jobs/in-All-Melbourne-VIC

IT Program Manager
https://www.seek.com.au/program-manager-jobs

IT Project jobs $120,000 $150,000
https://www.seek.com.au/it-project-manager-jobs

IT Project Management $60,000 $150,000
https://www.seek.com.au/learning/search/it-project-management-courses

IT Sales jobs $45,000 $180,000
https://www.seek.com.au/it-sales-jobs

IT Security Consultant $140,000
https://www.seek.com.au/cyber-security-consultant-jobs

IT Service Delivery $65,000 $122,000
https://www.seek.com.au/it-service-delivery-manager-jobs

IT Service Delivery Manager $65,000 $110,000
https://www.seek.com.au/it-service-delivery-manager-jobs

IT Software Development jobs $110,000 $120,000
https://www.seek.com.au/software-developer-jobs

IT Specialist $55,000 $85,000
https://www.seek.com.au/it-specialist-jobs

IT Support jobs $55,000 $66,000
https://www.seek.com.au/it-support-jobs

IT Support Technician $40,000 $90,000
https://www.seek.com.au/it-support-technician-jobs

IT System Administration jobs $55,000 $85,000
https://www.seek.com.au/system-administrator-jobs

IT Systems Engineer $70,000 $90,000
https://www.seek.com.au/systems-engineer-jobs

IT Tech jobs $50,000 $95,000
https://www.seek.com.au/it-technician-jobs

IT Trainee $35,000 $65,000
https://www.seek.com.au/it-trainee-jobs

IT Traineeships $35,000 $50,000
https://www.seek.com.au/it-traineeship-jobs/in-All-Melbourne-VIC

IT Trainer jobs $40,000 $85,000
https://www.seek.com.au/it-trainer-jobs

IT Vendor Manager $90,000
https://www.seek.com.au/it-vendor-manager-jobs

Java $110,000 $150,000
https://www.seek.com.au/java-jobs

Java Business Analyst $90,000 $150,000
https://www.seek.com.au/java-business-analyst-jobs

Javascript Developer $60,000 $140,000
https://www.seek.com.au/javascript-developer-jobs

Jobs Biotech $65,000 $70,000
https://www.seek.com.au/biotechnology-jobs

Junior Analyst $55,000 $80,000
https://www.seek.com.au/junior-analyst-jobs

Junior Business Intelligence $55,000
https://www.seek.com.au/junior-bi-jobs

Junior Developer $60,000 $80,000
https://www.seek.com.au/junior-developer-jobs

Junior Front End Developer $60,000 $80,000
https://www.seek.com.au/junior-front-end-developer-jobs

Junior IT jobs $35,000 $60,000
https://www.seek.com.au/junior-it-jobs

Junior Software Tester $60,000 $84,000
https://www.seek.com.au/junior-software-tester-jobs

Junior Test Analyst jobs $55,000 $84,000
https://www.seek.com.au/junior-test-analyst-jobs

Junior Tester jobs $55,000 $80,000
https://www.seek.com.au/junior-software-tester-jobs

Junior Web Developer $50,000 $80,000
https://www.seek.com.au/junior-web-developer-jobs

Library IT jobs $86,000 $96,000
https://www.seek.com.au/library-jobs

Linux jobs $120,000 $130,000
https://www.seek.com.au/linux-jobs

Machine Learning jobs $80,000 $160,000
https://www.seek.com.au/machine-learning-jobs

Mainframe jobs $100,000 $150,000
https://www.seek.com.au/mainframe-jobs

Media Communication jobs $70,000 $107,000
https://www.seek.com.au/media-communications-jobs

Microsoft Dynamics CRM Consultant $90,000 $120,000
https://www.seek.com.au/microsoft-dynamics-crm-jobs

Microsoft Dynamics CRM Developer $90,000 $200,000
https://www.seek.com.au/microsoft-dynamics-crm-jobs

NBN Installer jobs $60,000 $75,000
https://www.seek.com.au/nbn-installer-jobs

Microsoft.NET Developer $90,000 $150,000

https://www.seek.com.au/net-developer-jobs

Network Administrator $60,000 $105,000
https://www.seek.com.au/network-administrator-jobs

Network Analyst $96,000 $155,000
https://www.seek.com.au/network-analyst-jobs

Network Engineer $65,000 $150,000
https://www.seek.com.au/network-engineer-jobs

Network Security Roles $100,000 $140,000
https://www.seek.com.au/network-security-jobs

NGO IT jobs $55,000 $85,000
https://www.seek.com.au/ngo-jobs

NOC Engineer $65,000 $160,000
https://www.seek.com.au/noc-engineer-jobs

Oil and Gas IT jobs $95,000 $140,000
https://www.seek.com.au/oil-and-gas-jobs

Online Assistant $45,000 $50,000
https://www.seek.com.au/online-assistant-jobs

Online Data Entry jobs
https://www.seek.com.au/online-data-entry-jobs

Online jobs $45,000 $55,000
https://www.seek.com.au/work-from-home-jobs

Operations Analyst $70,000 $170,000
https://www.seek.com.au/operations-analyst-jobs

Operations Manager jobs $80,000 $150,000
https://www.seek.com.au/operations-manager-jobs

Oracle DBA Contract $110,000 $130,000
https://www.seek.com.au/oracle-dba-jobs/contract-temp

Part Time IT jobs $80,000 $95,000
https://www.seek.com.au/jobs-in-information-communication-technology/in-All-Sydney-NSW/part-time

PC Repair jobs $55,000 $70,000
https://www.seek.com.au/computer-repair-jobs

Performance Analyst$101,000 $140,000
https://www.seek.com.au/performance-analyst-jobs

Pre Sales Engineer $60,000 $150,000
https://www.seek.com.au/pre-sales-engineer-jobs

Process Analyst $90,000 $110,000
https://www.seek.com.au/process-analyst-jobs

Product Developer $80,000 $160,000
https://www.seek.com.au/product-developer-jobs

Product Engineer $110,000 $120,000
https://www.seek.com.au/product-engineer-jobs

Professional jobs $70,000 $126,000
https://www.seek.com.au/professional-services-jobs

Programming jobs $55,000 $150,000
https://www.seek.com.au/jobs-in-information-communication-technology/developers-programmers

Project Engineer jobs $90,000 $100,000
https://www.seek.com.au/jobs-in-engineering/project-engineering

Project Officer jobs $50,000 $75,000
https://www.seek.com.au/project-officer-jobs/in-All-Sydney-NSW

Python Jobs $70,000 $160,000
https://www.seek.com.au/python-jobs/in-All-Sydney-NSW

QA Officer $40,000 $70,000

https://www.seek.com.au/quality-assurance-officer-jobs

Quality Analyst $70,000 $90,000
https://www.seek.com.au/quality-analyst-jobs

Quality Control Manager $40,000 $85,000
https://www.seek.com.au/quality-control-manager-jobs

Quality Manager jobs $95,000 $110,000
https://www.seek.com.au/quality-manager-jobs

React Developer $70,000 $160,000
https://www.seek.com.au/react-js-jobs

Remote IT jobs $50,000 $80,000
https://www.seek.com.au/work-remotely-jobs

Research Analyst jobs $50,000 $96,000
https://www.seek.com.au/research-analyst-jobs

Research Assistant jobs $50,000 $85,000
https://www.seek.com.au/research-assistant-jobs

SAAS Sales Career $60,000 $170,000
https://www.seek.com.au/saas-sales-jobs

Salesforce Administrator $100,000 $120,000
https://www.seek.com.au/salesforce-administrator-jobs

Salesforce Consultant $110,000 $200,000
https://www.seek.com.au/salesforce-consultant-jobs

SAP BI Analyst $90,000 $111,000
https://www.seek.com.au/sap-business-intelligence-jobs

SAP CRM jobs $70,000 $90,000
https://www.seek.com.au/sap-crm-jobs

SAP Functional Consultant $100,000 $111,000
https://www.seek.com.au/sap-functional-consultant-jobs

SAP jobs $90,000 $130,000
https://www.seek.com.au/SAP-jobs

SAP Planner jobs $85,000 $95,000
https://www.seek.com.au/sap-planner-jobs

SAP Procurement jobs $100,000 $110,000
https://www.seek.com.au/sap-procurement-jobs

SAP Security jobs $80,000 $111,000
https://www.seek.com.au/sap-security-jobs

SAP Specialist $110,000 $130,000
https://www.seek.com.au/sap-specialist-jobs

SCADA Engineer $120,000
https://www.seek.com.au/scada-engineer-jobs

Security Manager jobs $75,000 $121,000
https://www.seek.com.au/security-manager-jobs

Security Operations Manager $75,000 $170,000
https://www.seek.com.au/security-operations-manager-jobs

Select Solutions jobs $85,000 $110,000
https://www.seek.com.au/Select-Solutions-jobs

Senior Data Analyst $85,000 $95,000
https://www.seek.com.au/senior-data-analyst-jobs/full-time

Senior Designer $50,000 $110,000
https://www.seek.com.au/senior-designer-jobs

SEO Manager $55,000 $140,000
https://www.seek.com.au/seo-manager-jobs

Service Desk jobs $50,000 $85,000
https://www.seek.com.au/service-desk-jobs

Service Technician jobs $50,000 $75,000
https://www.seek.com.au/field-service-technician-jobs

SharePoint jobs $80,000 $170,000
https://www.seek.com.au/sharepoint-jobs

SharePoint Specialist$80,000 $120,000
https://www.seek.com.au/sharepoint-consultant-jobs

Site Admin jobs $75,000
https://www.seek.com.au/site-administrator-jobs

Social Media jobs $50,000 $120,000
https://www.seek.com.au/social-media-jobs

Social Media Manager $55,000 $100,000
https://www.seek.com.au/social-media-manager-jobs

Software Engineer $60,000 $140,000
https://www.seek.com.au/software-engineer-jobs

Software Engineering Manager $130,000 $200,000
https://www.seek.com.au/software-engineering-manager-jobs

Software Programmer $70,000 $140,000
https://www.seek.com.au/software-developer-jobs

Software Sales $70,000 $150,000
https://www.seek.com.au/software-sales-jobs

Software Technology jobs $60,000 $110,000
https://www.seek.com.au/software-jobs

Software Test Engineer $80,000 $160,000
https://www.seek.com.au/test-engineer-jobs

Solidworks jobs $70,000 $75,000
https://www.seek.com.au/solidworks-jobs

Solution Architect Contract jobs

https://www.seek.com.au/solution-architect-jobs/contract-temp

Solution Architect jobs $100,000 $195,000
https://www.seek.com.au/solution-architect-jobs

Solutions Engineer $100,000 $150,000
https://www.seek.com.au/solutions-engineer-jobs

SQL $70,000 $150,000
https://www.seek.com.au/sql-jobs

SQL Data Analyst $55,000 $150,000
https://www.seek.com.au/sql-data-analyst-jobs

SQL Database Developer $80,000 $125,000
https://www.seek.com.au/database-developer-jobs

Starter IT jobs $50,000 $80,000
https://www.seek.com.au/entry-level-jobs

Strategic Planning Careers $67,000 $130,000
https://www.seek.com.au/strategic-planning-jobs

Strategy Manager $120,000 $220,000
https://www.seek.com.au/strategy-manager-jobs

Support Tech $50,000 $65,000
https://www.seek.com.au/learning/careers/it-support-technician

Tech Design jobs $75,000 $150,000
https://www.seek.com.au/Tech-Design-jobs

Tech Support jobs from Home $50,000
https://www.seek.com.au/jobs-in-information-communication-technology/help-desk-it-support/part-time

Technical Architect $70,000 $130,000
https://www.seek.com.au/technical-architect-jobs

Technical Writer jobs $70,000

https://www.seek.com.au/technical-writer-jobs/in-All-Sydney-NSW

Technology Job search $40,000 $300,000
https://www.seek.com.au/jobs-in-information-communication-technology

Telecom Engineer $60,000 $145,000
https://www.seek.com.au/telecommunication-engineer-jobs

Telstra jobs $40,000 $80,000
https://www.seek.com.au/Telstra-jobs/in-Townsville-QLD-4810

Test Analyst $70,000 $90,000
https://www.seek.com.au/test-analyst-jobs

Test Manager $70,000 $133,000
https://www.seek.com.au/test-manager-jobs

Trainee Project Manager jobs $80,000 $90,000
https://www.seek.com.au/trainee-project-manager-jobs

UAV jobs $45,000 $180,000
https://www.seek.com.au/uav-jobs

UI Designer $45,000 $100,000
https://www.seek.com.au/ui-designer-jobs

University IT jobs $27,000 $108,000
https://www.seek.com.au/university-jobs

User Experience jobs$87,000 $130,000
https://www.seek.com.au/user-experience-jobs

Video Editing work $60,000 $90,000
https://www.seek.com.au/video-editor-jobs

Web Analyst$90,000 $130,000
https://www.seek.com.au/web-analyst-jobs

Web Design jobs $55,000 $75,000

https://www.seek.com.au/web-design-jobs

Web Developer Graphics Designer $40,000 $70,000
https://www.seek.com.au/graphic-web-designer-jobs

Web Developer jobs $60,000 $100,000
https://www.seek.com.au/web-developer-jobs

Web Producer
https://www.seek.com.au/web-producer-jobs

Wireless Technician $81,000 $130,000
https://www.seek.com.au/wireless-technician-jobs

7 SEEK IT ROLES BY POPULARITY (AUSTRALIA)

This shows IT Roles by Internet traffic in descending order. Which IT Role phrases are the most popular?

Online Jobs, Cyber Security Jobs, Data Analyst Jobs, Network Administrator, Business Analyst Jobs, Freelance Graphic Designer Melbourne, Operations Manager Jobs, Test Analyst, Agile Business Analyst, iOS Developer Melbourne, IT Business Analyst, IT Specialist, Product Engineer, SEO Manager, Social Media Manager Jobs, Web Design Jobs, Web Developer Jobs, Digital Marketing Specialist, Entry Level IT Jobs Melbourne, Food Technology Jobs, Solutions Engineer, Technical Architect, Google Jobs Brisbane, IT Help Desk Jobs, NBN Installer Jobs, Process Analyst, Professional Jobs, Salesforce Administrator, Test Manager, Jobs C, C Software Engineer, Chief Engineer Jobs, Data Curation Jobs, Data Entry Career, Data Visualization Jobs, Senior Business Development Manager Jobs, Digital Architect Jobs, Digital Design AU, Entry Level Cisco Jobs, Hp Technical Support Jobs, IT Jobs With No Experience Required, IT Software Development Jobs, Java Business Analyst, Junior Business Intelligence, Microsoft Dynamics CRM Developer, Network Security Roles, Oracle DBA Contract, Part Time IT Jobs, Part Time PC Repair Jobs, SAP Procurement Jobs, Select Solutions Jobs, Software Engineering Manager, Software Test Engineer, SQL Australia, Starter IT Jobs, Strategy Manager, Tech Design Jobs, Junior User Experience Jobs, Web Developer Graphic Designer, Wireless Technician, Analyst Jobs In Australia, Angular 2 Developer, Assistant Development Manager Brisbane, Business Administration Work, Business Intelligence

Graduate, Chief Officer Jobs, Computer Design Jobs, Computer Games Programming Jobs, Computer Security Jobs, Continuous Improvement Roles, Data Analytics Consulting Jobs, Data Entry Contract Jobs, Data Privacy Jobs, Database Developer Jobs, Digital Content Producer Melbourne, Drupal Web Developer Jobs, Entry Level Computer Science Jobs, Head Of IT, Health Network Jobs, ICT Manager Jobs, Information And Knowledge Management Jobs, Information Resource Management Jobs, Information Systems Business Analyst, IoT Consulting Jobs, IT Business Support Analyst, IT Sales Jobs, IT Support Jobs In Australia, IT Vendor Manager, Junior Test Analyst Jobs In Sydney, Junior Tester Jobs, Machine Learning Jobs Australia, Product Developer Jobs, Python Jobs Sydney, React Developer, SAAS Sales Career, SAP BI Analyst, Sap Functional Consultant Jobs, Best Sap Jobs, SharePoint Jobs In Australia, SharePoint Specialist, Software Technology Jobs, Solution Architect Contract Jobs, Strategic Planning Careers, Android Developer Australia Jobs, Business Information Systems Jobs, ERP Consultant, Internet Marketing Jobs, IT Assistant, Computer Assembly Jobs, Entrepreneur Jobs, IT Jobs In Banks, JavaScript Developer, Project Engineer Jobs, Remote IT Jobs, Computer Engineering Jobs, Contract IT Jobs From Home, Hyperion Jobs, Info Technology Jobs, IT Business Development, Contract IT Jobs From Home, IT Systems Engineer, Linux Jobs, Network Engineer Jobs, Quality Analyst, University Research Assistant Jobs, Asp Net Developer, Business Improvement Manager, Core Java Developer Jobs, CRM Jobs, Data Quality Jobs, Database Analyst Jobs, Design Engineer Jobs, eLearning Developer, Entry Level Business Analyst, Field Service Manager Jobs, Interface Jobs, IT Delivery Manager, IT Developer, IT Systems Administrator Jobs, IT Traineeships Melbourne, IT Trainer Jobs, Junior Analyst, Microsoft Dynamics CRM Consultant, Oil And Gas IT Jobs, QA Officer, Salesforce Consultant, Sap CRM Jobs In Australia, Sap Security Jobs, Technology Job Search, Telecom Engineer, UI Designer Jobs, Animation Jobs Australia, Associate Business Analyst, Bi Analyst, Business Improvement Specialist, Business Intelligence Jobs Sydney, Business Intelligence Manager, CIO Jobs, Cobol Jobs, Commercial Analyst Jobs, Computer Forensics Jobs, Computer Networking Jobs, Computer Operator Jobs, Computer Software Developer, Computer Technician Jobs, Contract Coding Companies, Contract Software Engineer, Control Systems Jobs, Corporate Governance Jobs, CRM Business Analyst, CRM Manager Jobs, Cyber Forensics Jobs, Data Administrator, Data Center Jobs, Data Jobs, Data Jobs From Home, Data Migration Specialist, Data Mining Australia, Database Administrator Jobs, Database Officer,

Desktop Support Analyst, Digital Forensics Jobs, Digital Marketing Coordinator, Digital Media Careers, Digital Product Manager, Ecommerce Jobs Sydney, Embedded Systems Australia, Entry Level Software Engineer Jobs, ETL Developer Jobs, Game Industry Jobs, Game Programmer Jobs, Graphic Design Jobs Australia, Home Based Computer Jobs, Information Analyst, Information And Technology Jobs, Information Manager, Information Officer, Information Technology Jobs Melbourne, Information Technology Management Jobs, Infosys Australia Jobs, Integration Specialist, Intelligence Analyst Jobs Australia, IT Consultant Jobs, IT Manager Jobs Melbourne, IT Program Manager, IT Project Jobs, IT Security Consultant, IT Service Delivery, IT Service Delivery Manager, IT Support Technician, IT Tech Jobs, IT Trainee, Java Developer Jobs, Jobs Biotech, Junior Developer, Junior Front End Developer, Junior IT Jobs, Junior Software Tester, Junior Web Designer, Library IT Jobs, Mainframe Jobs In Australia, Media Communications Jobs, Net Jobs, Network Analyst, Ngo IT Jobs, NOC Engineer, Online Assistant, Online Data Entry Work, Online Assistant, Online Data Entry Work, Performance Analyst, Pre Sales Engineer, Programming Jobs Sydney, Project Officer Jobs Sydney, Quality Control Manager, Quality Manager Jobs, Research Analyst Jobs, Sap Planner Jobs, Sap Specialist, Scada Engineer, Security Manager Jobs Australia, Security Operations Manager Jobs, Senior Data Analyst, Senior Designer, Service Desk Jobs, Service Technician Jobs, Site Admin Jobs, Social Media Jobs Australia, Software Engineer Australia, Software Programmer, Software Sales, Solidworks Jobs, Solution Architect Jobs, SQL Data Analyst, SQL Database Developer, Support Tech, Tech Support Jobs From Home, Technical Writer Jobs Sydney, Telstra Jobs Townsville, Trainee Project Manager Jobs, UAV Jobs, University It Jobs, Video Editing Work, Web Analyst, Web Producer

8 TOP 300+ ROLES IN IT ON INDEED (INTERNATIONAL)

Compare your IT Roles shortlist with roles listed here from Indeed. Click on the links to find all the vacancies under IT Roles of interest. The digital tool for this chapter is https://itjobsformula.com/indeed/

IT Role Keyword   URL

3d animation work

https://au.indeed.com/3d-Animation-jobs

Access VBA developer

https://www.indeed.com/q-Ms-Access-Vba-Developer-jobs.html

Amazon com

https://www.indeed.com/cmp/Amazon.com/jobs

Analytical skills

https://www.indeed.com/career-advice/resumes-cover-letters/analytical-skills

Android developer Sydney

https://au.indeed.com/Android-Developer-jobs-in-Sydney-NSW

Animation illustration jobs

https://www.indeed.com/q-Animation-Illustration-jobs.html

Animation studios Sydney

https://au.indeed.com/Animation-Studio-jobs-in-Sydney-NSW

API integration jobs

https://www.indeed.com/q-API-Integration-jobs.html

Apple certified mac technician jobs

https://www.indeed.com/q-Apple-Certified-Macintosh-Technician-jobs.html

Apple store

https://au.indeed.com/Apple-Store-jobs

ASP NET jobs in Sydney

https://au.indeed.com/Net-Developer-jobs-in-Sydney-NSW

Assistant IT manager

https://www.indeed.com/q-Assistant-IT-Manager-jobs.html

Associates degree in computer networking jobs

https://www.indeed.com/q-Computer-Networking-Associate-Degree-jobs.html

Automation project engineer job description

https://www.indeed.com/q-Automation-Project-Engineer-jobs.html

Azure consultant hourly rate

https://au.indeed.com/Azure-Consultant-jobs

BI Australia

https://au.indeed.com/Bi-Australia-jobs

Big data finance jobs

https://au.indeed.com/Big-Data-Finance-jobs

Business analyst internship

https://au.indeed.com/Business-Analyst-Internship-jobs

Business analyst salary

https://au.indeed.com/salaries/Business-Analyst-Salaries

Business analyst telecommute

https://www.indeed.com/q-Telecommute-Business-Analyst-jobs.html

Business consultant

https://au.indeed.com/Entry-Level-Business-Consultant-jobs

Cache developer

https://www.indeed.com/q-Intersystem-Cache-Developer-jobs.html

Catia v5 jobs in Canada

https://ca.indeed.com/CATIA-V5-jobs-in-Toronto,-ON

CCNA

https://au.indeed.com/CCNA-jobs

CCNA indeed

https://www.indeed.com/q-CCNA-jobs.html

CCNP data center jobs

https://www.indeed.com/q-Ccnp-Data-Center-jobs.html

Climate technologies

https://au.indeed.com/cmp/Climate-Technologies/reviews

Computational and applied mathematics jobs

https://www.indeed.com/q-Computational-Mathematics-jobs.html

Computer engineering salary

https://au.indeed.com/salaries/Computer-Engineer-Salaries

Computer forensics technician

https://www.indeed.com/q-Computer-Forensic-Technician-jobs.html

Computer jobs with no experience needed

https://au.indeed.com/No-Experience-Computer-jobs

Computer networking jobs in Melbourne

https://au.indeed.com/Computer-Networking-jobs-in-Melbourne-VIC

Computer repair

https://au.indeed.com/Computer-Repair-jobs-in-Sydney-NSW

Computer science internships

https://au.indeed.com/Computer-Science-Internship-jobs-in-Sydney-NSW

Computer skills

https://www.indeed.com/career-advice/resumes-cover-letters/computer-skills

Computer technician

https://au.indeed.com/Computer-Technician-jobs

Computer technology certificate jobs

https://au.indeed.com/Information-Technology-Certificate-jobs

Computer trainer

https://au.indeed.com/Computer-Trainer-jobs

Consultant sap junior

https://au.indeed.com/Junior-SAP-Consultant-jobs

Content creator

https://au.indeed.com/Social-Media-Content-Creator-jobs

Content writing work from home

https://au.indeed.com/Work-From-Home-Content-Writing-jobs

Control systems engineering

https://au.indeed.com/Control-Systems-Engineer-jobs

Copywriter

https://au.indeed.com/Copywriter-jobs

Creative digital marketing jobs

https://au.indeed.com/Creative-Marketing-jobs

CSIRO jobs

https://au.indeed.com/Csiro-jobs

CTO contract jobs

https://www.indeed.com/q-Contract-CTO-jobs.html

Customer logistics analyst

https://www.indeed.com/q-Customer-Logistics-Analyst-jobs.html

Cyber security jobs

https://au.indeed.com/Cyber-Security-jobs

Cyber security police jobs

https://au.indeed.com/Cyber-Crime-jobs

Cyber security software engineer

https://www.indeed.com/q-Cyber-Security-Software-Engineer-jobs.html

Cybernetics jobs

https://www.indeed.com/q-Cybernetics-jobs.html

Data analyst internship

https://au.indeed.com/Trainee,-Internship,-Data-Analyst,-Statistics-jobs

Data analyst jobs Atlanta

https://www.indeed.com/q-Data-Analyst-l-Atlanta,-GA-jobs.html

Data analyst salary

https://au.indeed.com/salaries/Data-Analyst-Salaries

Data entry

https://au.indeed.com/Data-Entry-jobs

Data entry jobs

https://au.indeed.com/Data-Entry-jobs-in-Sydney-NSW

Data entry jobs Melbourne

https://au.indeed.com/Data-Entry-jobs-in-Melbourne-VIC

Data entry jobs Melbourne work from home

https://au.indeed.com/Work-From-Home,-Data-Entry-jobs-in-Melbourne-VIC

Data entry jobs Sydney

https://au.indeed.com/Data-Entry-jobs-in-Sydney-NSW

Data entry jobs worldwide

https://www.indeed.com/q-Worldwide-Data-Entry-jobs.html

Data entry work from home

https://au.indeed.com/Data-Entry,-Work-From-Home-jobs

Data solutions architect

https://au.indeed.com/Big-Data-Solution-Architect-jobs

Data visualization Toronto

https://ca.indeed.com/Data-Visualization-jobs-in-Toronto,-ON

Database maintenance job description

https://www.indeed.com/q-Database-Maintenance-jobs.html

Dell EMC

https://au.indeed.com/Dell-EMC-jobs

Design jobs Canberra

https://au.indeed.com/Creative-Design-jobs-in-Canberra-ACT

Design student jobs

https://au.indeed.com/Graphic-Design-Student-jobs

Deskside support technician

https://www.indeed.com/q-Deskside-Support-Technician-jobs.html

Digital analytics analyst

https://www.indeed.com/q-Digital-Analytics-Analyst-jobs.html

Digital developer

https://au.indeed.com/Digital-Developer-jobs

Digital intermediate jobs

https://au.indeed.com/Digital-Intermediate-jobs-in-Sydney-NSW

Digital manufacturing jobs

https://www.indeed.com/q-Digital-Manufacturing-jobs.html

Digital marketing consultant

https://au.indeed.com/Digital-Marketing-Consultant-jobs-in-Melbourne-VIC

Digital marketing consultant

https://au.indeed.com/Digital-Marketing-Consultant-jobs

Digital marketing graphic designer job description

https://www.indeed.com/q-Digital-Marketing-Graphic-Designer-jobs.html

Digital marketing internship

https://au.indeed.com/Digital-Marketing-Internship-jobs

Digital marketing Victoria BC

https://ca.indeed.com/Digital-Marketing-jobs-in-Victoria,-BC

Digital strategy manager

https://au.indeed.com/Digital-Strategy-Manager-jobs

Digital web manager job description

https://www.indeed.com/q-Digital-Web-Manager-jobs.html

Digital work from home jobs

https://au.indeed.com/Work-From-Home-Digital,-Online-jobs

Director of new product development

https://www.indeed.com/q-Director-New-Product-Development-jobs.html

Dream jobs work from home

https://www.indeed.com/q-Work-Home-Dream-jobs.html

Embedded jobs in Canada

https://ca.indeed.com/Embedded-Software-Engineer-jobs

End user services manager job description

https://www.indeed.com/q-End-User-Service-Manager-jobs.html

ER tech jobs

https://www.indeed.com/q-Emergency-Room-Technician-jobs.html

Forensic science salary Australia

https://au.indeed.com/salaries/Forensic-Scientist-Salaries

Fortran developer jobs

https://www.indeed.com/q-Fortran-Developer-jobs.html

Freelance graphic designer Boston

https://www.indeed.com/q-Freelance-Graphic-Designer-l-Boston,-MA-jobs.html

Freelance jobs

https://au.indeed.com/Freelance-jobs

Front end developer

https://au.indeed.com/Front-End-Developer-jobs

Full stack designer salary

https://au.indeed.com/salaries/Full-Stack-Developer-Salaries

Full stack developer

https://au.indeed.com/Full-Stack-Developer-jobs

Full stack developer remote

https://www.indeed.com/q-Full-Stack-Developer-Remote-jobs.html

Full stack developer salary

https://au.indeed.com/salaries/Full-Stack-Developer-Salaries

Game studios Sydney

https://au.indeed.com/Game-Studio-jobs

Google Australia

https://au.indeed.com/Google-Australia-jobs

Google com a

https://au.indeed.com/Www-Google-Com-Au-jobs

Google jobs

https://au.indeed.com/Google-jobs-in-Sydney-NSW

Google jobs in Qatar

https://qa.indeed.com/Google-jobs-in-Doha

Graphic design Brisbane

https://au.indeed.com/Graphic-Designer-jobs-in-Brisbane-QLD

Graphic design for film jobs

https://au.indeed.com/Graphic-Designer-Film-jobs

Graphic design internship Melbourne

https://au.indeed.com/Design-Intern-jobs-in-Melbourne-VIC

Graphic design internship Sydney

https://au.indeed.com/Graphic-Design-Internship-jobs-in-Sydney-NSW

Graphic design jobs

https://au.indeed.com/Graphic-Designer-jobs-in-Sydney-NSW

Graphic designer job vacancy in Qatar

https://qa.indeed.com/Graphic-Designer-jobs

Healthcare business analyst

https://au.indeed.com/Healthcare-Business-Analyst-jobs

HFC technician salary

https://au.indeed.com/Nbn-Hfc-jobs

IBM Ballarat

https://au.indeed.com/IBM-jobs-in-Ballarat-VIC

IBM help desk jobs

https://www.indeed.com/q-Help-Desk-Support-IBM-jobs.html

IBM jobs Florida

https://www.indeed.com/q-IBM-l-Florida-jobs.html

IBM jobs Texas

https://www.indeed.com/q-IBM-l-Texas-jobs.html

IBM ODM developer

https://www.indeed.com/q-IBM-Odm-Developer-Rule-Developer-jobs.html

IBM part time

https://au.indeed.com/IBM-Part-Time-jobs

IBM solution architect

https://au.indeed.com/IBM-Solutions-Architect-jobs

ICT architect

https://au.indeed.com/Ict-Architect-jobs-in-Sydney-NSW

Illustrator jobs Sydney

https://au.indeed.com/Illustrator-jobs-in-Sydney-NSW

Indeed computer science internship

https://au.indeed.com/Computer-Science-Internship-jobs-in-Sydney-NSW

Indeed SAP basis jobs

https://au.indeed.com/SAP-Basis-jobs

Indie game audio jobs

https://www.indeed.com/q-Game-Audio-jobs.html

Information literacy librarian

https://www.indeed.com/q-Information-Literacy-Librarian-jobs.html

Information technology developer

https://www.indeed.com/q-Information-Technology-Developer-jobs.html

Innovation development manager

https://www.indeed.com/q-Innovation-Development-Manager-jobs.html

Intelligence gathering jobs

https://www.indeed.com/q-Intelligence-Gathering-jobs.html

Internal quality assurance jobs

https://au.indeed.com/Internal-Auditor-Quality-Assurance-jobs

Internet based jobs from home

https://au.indeed.com/Online-Home-Based-jobs

Internet research jobs from home

https://au.indeed.com/Work-At-Home,-Internet-Research-jobs

Intuit business data analyst

https://www.indeed.com/q-Business-Data-Analyst-Intuit-jobs.html

iOS developer Brisbane

https://au.indeed.com/Ios-Developer-jobs-in-Brisbane-QLD

iPhone developer Melbourne

https://au.indeed.com/Ios-Developer-jobs-in-Melbourne-VIC

IT apprenticeships

https://au.indeed.com/IT-Apprenticeship-jobs-in-Sydney-NSW

IT asset management analyst job description

https://www.indeed.com/q-IT-Asset-Management-Analyst-jobs.html

IT companies in Adelaide

https://au.indeed.com/IT-jobs-in-Adelaide-SA

IT contractor

https://au.indeed.com/IT-Contractor-jobs

IT development program

https://www.indeed.com/q-IT-Development-Program-Associate-jobs.html

IT internship Melbourne

https://au.indeed.com/IT-Internship-jobs

IT internships

https://au.indeed.com/IT-Internship-jobs-in-Sydney-NSW

IT internships Sydney

https://au.indeed.com/IT-Internship-jobs-in-Sydney-NSW

IT job

https://au.indeed.com/IT-jobs-in-Melbourne-VIC

IT jobs

https://au.indeed.com/IT-jobs-in-Sydney-NSW

IT jobs Adelaide

https://au.indeed.com/IT-jobs-in-Adelaide-SA

IT jobs Boston MA

https://www.indeed.com/l-Boston,-MA-jobs.html

IT jobs Green Bay

https://www.indeed.com/q-Information-Technology-l-Green-Bay,-WI-jobs.html

IT jobs in Texas

https://www.indeed.com/q-IT-Specialist-l-Texas-jobs.html

IT jobs Melbourne

https://au.indeed.com/IT-jobs-in-Melbourne-VIC

IT jobs Melbourne

https://au.indeed.com/No-Experience-IT-jobs-in-Melbourne-VIC

IT jobs MN

https://www.indeed.com/q-IT-Specialist-I-Minnesota-jobs.html

IT jobs Sydney

https://au.indeed.com/IT-jobs-in-Sydney-NSW

IT jobs Sydney

https://au.indeed.com/Entry-Level-IT-jobs-in-Sydney-NSW

IT networking internship

https://au.indeed.com/Networking-Internship-jobs

IT officer

https://au.indeed.com/IT-Officer-jobs

IT onsite support

https://au.indeed.com/IT-Onsite-Support-jobs-in-Sydney-NSW

IT project manager jobs in Qatar

https://qa.indeed.com/IT-Project-Manager-jobs-in-Doha

IT security jobs in USA
https://www.indeed.com/jobs?q=cyber+security&l=USA&rbc=Raytheon
&jcid=aa53b551f9df0210

IT site manager

https://www.indeed.com/q-IT-Site-Manager-jobs.html

IT specialist Melbourne

https://au.indeed.com/IT-Specialist-jobs-in-Melbourne-VIC

IT support

https://au.indeed.com/IT-Support-jobs

IT support Melbourne

https://au.indeed.com/IT-Support-jobs-in-Melbourne-VIC

IT support Portland

https://www.indeed.com/q-IT-Support-I-Portland,-OR-jobs.html

IT support Sydney

https://au.indeed.com/IT-Support-jobs-in-Sydney-NSW

IT worker

https://www.indeed.com/q-IT-Worker-jobs.html

IT works jobs

https://www.indeed.com/cmp/IT-Works

Java developer positions

https://au.indeed.com/Java-Developer-jobs

Java jobs in Canada

https://ca.indeed.com/Java-Developer-jobs

JDE technical

https://www.indeed.com/q-Jde-Technical-Developer-jobs.html

Jobs for computer science students

https://au.indeed.com/Computer-Science-Student-Jobs-jobs

Junior online

https://au.indeed.com/Junior-Online-jobs-in-New-South-Wales

Lead business systems analyst job description

https://www.indeed.com/q-Lead-Business-Systems-Analyst-jobs.html

Lims administrator

https://www.indeed.com/q-Lims-Administrator-jobs.html

Mac IT jobs

https://au.indeed.com/Mac-IT-Support-jobs-in-Melbourne-VIC

Magento developer Melbourne

https://au.indeed.com/Magento-Developer-jobs-in-Melbourne-VIC

Magento developer Sydney

https://au.indeed.com/Magento-Developer-jobs-in-Sydney-NSW

Marketing jobs

https://au.indeed.com/Marketing-jobs

Marketing web developer job description

https://www.indeed.com/q-Marketing-Web-Developer-jobs.html

Media internships Sydney

https://au.indeed.com/Media-Internships-jobs-in-Sydney-NSW

Media jobs Victoria BC

https://ca.indeed.com/Media-jobs-in-Victoria,-BC

Medical technologist

https://au.indeed.com/salaries/Medical-Technologist-Salaries

Metrics reporting analyst job description

https://www.indeed.com/q-Metrics-Reporting-Analyst-jobs.html

Music software developer

https://www.indeed.com/q-Audio-Music-Software-Engineer-jobs.html

MySQL database developer

https://www.indeed.com/q-MySQL-Database-Developer-jobs.html

NASA cyber security internship

https://www.indeed.com/q-Nasa-Nasa-IT-Security-jobs.html

NET developer Sydney

https://au.indeed.com/Net-Developer-jobs-in-Sydney-NSW

Network engineer

https://au.indeed.com/Network-Engineer-jobs

Network engineer

https://au.indeed.com/Cisco-Network-Engineer-jobs

Network support technician

https://au.indeed.com/Network-Support-Technician-jobs

Offsite graphic designer wanted

https://www.indeed.com/q-Offsite-Graphic-Designer-jobs.html

Online bookkeeping jobs

https://au.indeed.com/Online-Bookkeeping-jobs

Online data entry jobs

https://au.indeed.com/Work-From-Home,-Data-Entry-jobs

Online internships for college students

https://www.indeed.com/q-Online-Internship-jobs.html

Online jobs

https://au.indeed.com/Work-From-Home-jobs

Online jobs from home

https://au.indeed.com/Work-Home-Online-jobs

Online marketing internships

https://au.indeed.com/Digital-Marketing-Internship-jobs

Online teaching jobs

https://au.indeed.com/Online-Teaching-jobs

Online teaching jobs Australia

https://au.indeed.com/Online-Teaching-jobs

Online tech support jobs work from home

https://au.indeed.com/Work-At-Home-Technical-Support-jobs

Online tutoring jobs

https://au.indeed.com/Online-Tutor-jobs

Online tutoring jobs

https://au.indeed.com/Online-Tutor-jobs-in-Sydney-NSW

Online work from home

https://au.indeed.com/Work-Home-Online-jobs

Optical network engineer job description

https://www.indeed.com/q-Optical-Network-Engineer-jobs.html

Oracle apps jobs in USA

https://www.indeed.com/q-Oracle-Ebs-jobs.html

Oracle database engineer

https://www.indeed.com/q-Oracle-Database-Engineer-jobs.html

PC hardware technician

https://au.indeed.com/Computer-Hardware-Technician-jobs

PC hardware technician jobs

https://au.indeed.com/Computer-Hardware-Technician-jobs

Performance management consultant job description

https://www.indeed.com/q-Performance-Management-Consultant-jobs.html

Perl developer salary

https://au.indeed.com/Perl-Developer-jobs

PHP developer jobs in Sydney

https://au.indeed.com/PHP-Developer-jobs-in-Sydney-NSW

Placement websites

https://www.indeed.com/q-Next-Placement-Website-jobs.html

POS designer jobs

https://au.indeed.com/Pos-Designer-jobs

PPC expert jobs

https://au.indeed.com/PPC-Specialist-jobs

Principal business systems analyst job description

https://www.indeed.com/q-Principal-Business-Systems-Analyst-jobs.html

Problem solving skills

https://www.indeed.com/career-advice/resumes-cover-letters/problem-solving-skills

Programmed

https://au.indeed.com/Programmed-jobs

Project engineer

https://au.indeed.com/Project-Engineer-jobs-in-South-Australia

Python Django developer

https://au.indeed.com/Python-Django-Developer-jobs

R&D project manager

https://au.indeed.com/R&D-Project-Manager-jobs

Real telecommute jobs

https://www.indeed.com/q-Real-Telecommute-jobs.html

Remote help desk support

https://www.indeed.com/q-Remote-Helpdesk-Support-jobs.html

Remote UI UX jobs

https://www.indeed.com/q-Remote-Ui-Ux-Designer-jobs.html

Responsive web design jobs

https://www.indeed.com/q-Responsive-Web-Designer-jobs.html

Ruby programming jobs

https://www.indeed.com/q-Ruby-Programmer-jobs.html

Salesforce database administrator

https://www.indeed.com/q-Salesforce-Database-Administrator-jobs.html

SAP basis work from home jobs

https://www.indeed.com/q-SAP-Basis-I-Work-At-Home-jobs.html

SAP Hybris jobs in USA

https://www.indeed.com/q-SAP-Hybris-jobs.html

Satellite technician

https://au.indeed.com/Satellite-Technician-jobs

SCADA network engineer

https://www.indeed.com/q-Scada-Network-Engineer-jobs.html

Scope of computer science in Australia

https://au.indeed.com/Computer-Science-jobs

SDN developer

https://www.indeed.com/q-Sdn-Developer-jobs.html

Senior digital marketing manager

https://au.indeed.com/Senior-Digital-Marketing-Manager-jobs

Senior field technician

https://au.indeed.com/Senior-Field-Technician-jobs-in-Western-Australia

Senior information security consultant

https://au.indeed.com/Senior-Security-Consultant-jobs

Senior integration engineer job description

https://www.indeed.com/q-Senior-Integration-Engineer-jobs.html

Senior NOC engineer job description

https://www.indeed.com/q-Senior-Noc-Engineer-jobs.html

Senior social media manager job description

https://www.indeed.com/q-Senior-Social-Media-Manager-jobs.html

Senior Tableau developer

https://www.indeed.com/q-Senior-Tableau-Developer-jobs.html

SEO specialist

https://au.indeed.com/SEO-Specialist-jobs

Server support engineer salary

https://au.indeed.com/Server-Support-Engineer-jobs-in-Victoria

Service level manager jobs

https://au.indeed.com/Itil-Service-Level-Manager-jobs

Service virtualization jobs

https://au.indeed.com/CA-Devtest,-Service-Virtualization-jobs-in-Melbourne-VIC

ServiceNow jobs in Canada

https://ca.indeed.com/Servicenow-jobs

SharePoint

https://au.indeed.com/Sharepoint-jobs

SharePoint solution architect

https://www.indeed.com/q-Sharepoint-Solution-Architect-jobs.html

Siemens

https://au.indeed.com/Siemens-jobs

Site admin jobs Alberta

https://ca.indeed.com/Site-Administrator-jobs-in-Alberta

Social media content evaluator

https://www.indeed.com/q-Social-Media-Content-Evaluation-Specialist-jobs.html

Social media content moderator

https://www.indeed.com/q-Social-Media-Moderator-jobs.html

Social media intern

https://au.indeed.com/Social-Media-Intern-jobs-in-Sydney-NSW

Social media jobs

https://au.indeed.com/Social-Media-jobs-in-Sydney-NSW

Social media manager

https://au.indeed.com/Social-Media-Manager-jobs

Software companies in Brisbane

https://au.indeed.com/Software-Companies-jobs-in-Brisbane-QLD

Software companies in Victoria BC

https://ca.indeed.com/One-Software-Company-jobs-in-Victoria,-BC

Software deployment engineer job description

https://www.indeed.com/q-Software-Deployment-Engineer-jobs.html

Software developer

https://au.indeed.com/Software-Developer-jobs-in-Melbourne-VIC

Software developer

https://au.indeed.com/Software-Developer-jobs

Software engineer internship

https://au.indeed.com/Internship-Software-Engineering-jobs

Software engineer jobs Austin

https://www.indeed.com/q-Software-Engineer-I-Austin,-TX-jobs.html

Software engineer summer intern

https://au.indeed.com/Internship-Software-Engineering-jobs

Software engineer travel jobs

https://www.indeed.com/q-Software-Engineer-World-Travel-jobs.html

Software project leader

https://www.indeed.com/q-Software-Project-Leader-jobs.html

Software research jobs

https://www.indeed.com/q-Software-Research-jobs.html

Solution architect

https://au.indeed.com/Solution-Architect-jobs

Strategy and business development analyst

https://www.indeed.com/q-Corporate-Strategy-Business-Development-Analyst-jobs.html

System administrator

https://au.indeed.com/System-Administrator-jobs

System support technician job description

https://www.indeed.com/q-System-Support-Technician-jobs.html

Tech companies Sydney

https://au.indeed.com/Tech-Company-jobs-in-Sydney-NSW

Tech jobs with no experience

https://au.indeed.com/No-Experience-Information-Technology-jobs

Techforce

https://au.indeed.com/Techforce-jobs

Technical document controller

https://www.indeed.com/q-Technical-Document-Control-Specialist-jobs.html

Technical marketing consultant

https://www.indeed.com/q-Technical-Marketing-Consultant-jobs.html

Technical writer jobs Austin

https://www.indeed.com/q-Technical-Writer-I-Austin,-TX-jobs.html

Technology assistant jobs

https://au.indeed.com/Technology-Assistant-jobs-in-Melbourne-VIC

Technology sales consultant

https://www.indeed.com/q-Technology-Sales-Consultant-jobs.html

Telecom consulting jobs

https://au.indeed.com/Telecommunication-Consultant-jobs

Telecom project engineer

https://au.indeed.com/Telecommunications-Project-Engineer-jobs

Telecom strategy jobs

https://www.indeed.com/q-Telecom-Strategy-jobs.html

Telecommunications technician

https://au.indeed.com/Telecommunications-Technician-jobs

Telecommute customer service jobs

https://www.indeed.com/q-Telecommuting-Customer-Service-jobs.html

Telecommuting technology jobs

https://www.indeed.com/q-Telecommute-Tech-jobs.html

Telework jobs from home

https://au.indeed.com/Work-From-Home-,-Telecommute-jobs

Telstra careers

https://au.indeed.com/Telstra-jobs-in-Melbourne-VIC

Telstra media

https://au.indeed.com/Telstra-Media-jobs

Test architect jobs

https://au.indeed.com/Test-Architect-jobs

Test design engineer

https://www.indeed.com/q-Test-Design-Engineer-jobs.html

Transaction analyst

https://au.indeed.com/Transaction-Analyst-jobs

Transcription jobs

https://au.indeed.com/Transcription-jobs

UI design internship

https://au.indeed.com/Ux,-Ui,-Intern-jobs

Unity software engineer

https://www.indeed.com/q-Unity-Software-Engineer-jobs.html

UX design Sydney

https://au.indeed.com/Ux-Designer-jobs-in-Sydney-NSW

UX internship Sydney

https://au.indeed.com/User-Experience-Internship-jobs-in-Sydney-NSW

UX specialist jobs

https://au.indeed.com/Ux-Specialist-jobs

UX writer jobs

https://au.indeed.com/Ux-Writer-jobs

Video game internships

https://www.indeed.com/q-Video-Game-Intern-jobs.html

Virtual assistant jobs

https://au.indeed.com/Virtual-Assistant-jobs

Virtual technical writer

https://www.indeed.com/q-Virtual-Technical-Writer-jobs.html

Virtual writing jobs

https://www.indeed.com/q-Virtual-Writing-jobs.html

VP IT jobs

https://au.indeed.com/VP-Technology-jobs-in-Sydney-NSW

VR internship

https://www.indeed.com/q-Virtual-Reality-Intern-jobs.html

Web application development jobs

https://au.indeed.com/Web-Application-Developer-jobs

Web designer job in USA

https://www.indeed.com/q-Web-Designer-l-New-York,-NY-jobs.html

Web developer

https://au.indeed.com/Web-Developer-jobs

Web developer Calgary

https://ca.indeed.com/Web-Developer-jobs-in-Calgary,-AB

Web developer California

https://www.indeed.com/q-Web-Developer-l-California-jobs.html

Web developer jobs Dublin

https://ie.indeed.com/Web-Developer-jobs-in-Dublin

Web developer Melbourne

https://au.indeed.com/Web-Developer-jobs-in-Melbourne-VIC

Wellington tech jobs

https://nz.indeed.com/IT-Tech-jobs-in-Wellington-City,-Wellington

Wireless system engineer

https://www.indeed.com/q-Wireless-Systems-Engineer-jobs.html

Wix designer jobs

https://www.indeed.com/q-Wix-Designer-jobs.html

work from home Australia

https://au.indeed.com/Work-From-Home-jobs

Work from home software testing jobs

https://au.indeed.com/Work-From-Home-Software-Testing-jobs

Working at Microsoft store

https://au.indeed.com/Microsoft-Store-jobs

Working from home

https://au.indeed.com/Work-From-Home-jobs-in-New-South-Wales

ZOHO CRM jobs

https://www.indeed.com/q-Zoho-Crm-jobs.html

9 INDEED (INTERNATIONAL) IT ROLES BY POPULARITY

This shows IT Roles by Internet traffic in descending order. Which IT Role phrases are the most popular?

Apple Store, Google Australia, Telstra Media, SharePoint, Amazon Com, Programmed, BI Australia, Computer Repair, Copywriter, Online Jobs, Google Jobs, Web Developer, CSIRO Jobs, Telstra Jobs, CCNA, IT Support, Social Media Manager, Working From Home, Software Developer, Analytical Skills, Business Consultant, Full Stack Developer, IT Support Melbourne, Climate Technologies, Dell EMC, Graphic Design Jobs, Solution Architect, Transcription Jobs, Virtual Assistant Jobs, Control Systems Engineering, Cyber Security Jobs, Entity Solutions, Marketing Jobs, Siemens, Google Com A, Graphic Design Brisbane, Network Engineer, Network Engineer, Project Engineer, System Administrator, Techforce, Computer Technician, Data Entry Jobs Sydney, Data Entry Work From Home, Front End Developer, Online Data Entry Jobs, Telecommunications Technician, IT Jobs Sydney, IT Jobs Melbourne, IT Jobs Melbourne, IT Jobs Sydney, IT Jobs Sydney, IT Support Sydney, Online Jobs From Home, SEO Specialist, Social Media Jobs, Online Tutoring Jobs, Online Work From Home, Animation Studios Sydney, Digital Marketing Consultant, Freelance Jobs Australia, IBM Ballarat, IT Jobs Adelaide, IT Onsite Support, Online Tutoring Australia,

Web Developer Melbourne, IT Internship Melbourne, IT Internships Sydney, Web Developer Brisbane, Business Analyst Internship, Social Media Content Creator, Graphic Design Internship Sydney, iOS Developer Brisbane, It Apprenticeships, It Companies In Adelaide, IT Job, Junior Online, Software Engineer Internship, Tech Companies Sydney, Android Developer Sydney, ER Tech Jobs, ICT Architect, iPhone Developer Melbourne, IT Contractor, Magento Developer Melbourne, Media Internships, Online Bookkeeping Jobs, Software Companies In Brisbane, UX Design Sydney, Data Analyst Internship, Data Entry Jobs Melbourne Work From Home, Digital Marketing Internship, Game Studios Sydney, Online Teaching Jobs Australia, Social Media Intern, 3d Animation Work, Access VBA Developer, Animation Illustration Jobs, API Integration Jobs, Apple Certified Mac Technician Jobs, Asp Net Jobs In Sydney, Assistant IT Manager, Associates Degree In Computer Networking Jobs, Automation Project Engineer Job Description, Azure Consultant Jobs, Big Data Finance Jobs, Business Analyst Telecommute, Cache Developer, Catia V5 Jobs In Canada, CCNA Indeed, CCNP Data Center Jobs, Computational And Applied Mathematics Jobs, Computer Forensics Technician, Computer Jobs With No Experience Needed, Computer Networking Jobs In Melbourne, Computer Technology Certificate Jobs, Computer Trainer, Consultant Sap Junior, Content Writing Work From Home, Creative Digital Marketing Jobs, CTO Contract Jobs, Customer Logistics Analyst, Cyber Security Police Jobs, Cyber Security Software Engineer, Cybernetics Jobs, Data Analyst Jobs Atlanta, Data Entry Jobs Worldwide, Data Solutions Architect, Data Visualization Toronto, Database Maintenance Job Description, Design Jobs Canberra, Design Student Jobs, Deskside Support Technician, Digital Analytics Analyst, Digital Developer, Digital Intermediate Jobs, Digital Manufacturing Jobs, Digital Marketing Graphic Designer Job Description, Digital Marketing Victoria BC, Digital Strategy Manager, Digital Web Manager Job Description, Digital Work From Home Jobs, Director Of New Product Development, Dream Jobs Work From Home, Embedded Jobs In Canada, End User Services Manager Job Description, Fortran Developer Jobs, Freelance Graphic Designer Boston, Full Stack Developer Remote, Google Jobs In Qatar, Graphic Design For Film Jobs, Paid Graphic Design Internships, Graphic Designer Job Vacancy In Qatar, Healthcare Business Analyst, HFC Technician Salary, IBM Help Desk Jobs,

IBM Jobs Florida, IBM Jobs Texas, IBM ODM Developer, IBM Part Time, IBM Solution Architect, Illustrator Jobs Sydney, Indeed Sap Basis Jobs, Indie Game Audio Jobs, Information Literacy Librarian, Information Technology Developer, Innovation Development Manager, Intelligence Gathering Jobs, Internal Quality Assurance Jobs, Internet Based Jobs From Home, Internet Research Jobs From Home, Intuit Business Data Analyst, IT Asset Management Analyst Job Description, IT Development Program, IT Jobs Green Bay, IT Jobs In Texas, IT Jobs Mn, IT Networking Internship, IT Officer, IT Project Manager Jobs In Qatar, IT Site Manager, IT Specialist Melbourne, IT Support Portland, IT Worker, Java Developer Positions, Java Jobs In Canada, JDE Technical, Jobs For Computer Science Students, Lead Business Systems Analyst Job Description, Lims Administrator, Mac It Jobs, Magento Developer Sydney, Marketing Web Developer Job Description, Media Jobs Victoria BC, Metrics Reporting Analyst Job Description, Music Software Developer, MySQL Database Developer, Nasa Cyber Security Internship, Net Developer Sydney, Network Support Technician, Offsite Graphic Designer Wanted, Online Internships For College Students, Online Marketing Internships, Online Tech Support Jobs Work From Home, Optical Network Engineer Job Description, Oracle Apps Jobs In USA, Oracle Database Engineer, Pc Hardware Technician Jobs, Performance Management Consultant Job Description, Php Developer Jobs In Sydney, Placement Websites, POS Designer Jobs, PPC Expert Jobs, Principal Business Systems Analyst Job Description, Python Django Developer, R&D Project Manager, Real Telecommute Jobs, Remote Help Desk Support, Remote UI UX Jobs, Responsive Web Design Jobs, Ruby Programming Jobs, Salesforce Database Administrator, Indeed Sap Basis Jobs, Sap Hybris Jobs In USA, Satellite Technician, Scada Network Engineer, Scope Of Computer Science In Australia, SDN Developer, Senior Digital Marketing Manager, Senior Field Technician, Senior Information Security Consultant, Senior Integration Engineer Job Description, Senior NOC Engineer Job Description, Senior Social Media Manager Job Description, Senior Tableau Developer, Service Level Manager Jobs, Service Virtualization Jobs, ServiceNow Jobs In Canada, SharePoint Solution Architect, Site Admin Jobs Alberta, Social Media Content Moderator, Social Media Content Evaluator, Software Companies In Victoria BC, Software Deployment Engineer Job Description, Software Engineer Jobs Austin,

Software Engineer Summer Intern, Software Engineer Travel Jobs, Software Project Leader, Software Research Jobs, Strategy And Business Development Analyst, System Support Technician Job Description, Tech Jobs With No Experience, Technical Document Controller, Technical Marketing Consultant, Technical Writer Jobs Austin, Technology Assistant Jobs, Technology Sales Consultant, Telecom Consulting Jobs, Telecom Project Engineer, Telecom Strategy Jobs, Telecommute Customer Service Jobs, Telecommuting Technology Jobs, Test Architect Jobs, Test Design Engineer, Transaction Analyst, Types Of Database Jobs, UI Design Internship, Unity Software Engineer, UX Internship Sydney, UX Specialist Jobs, UX Writer Jobs, Video Game Internships, Virtual Technical Writer, Virtual Writing Jobs, VP IT Jobs, VR Internship, Web Application Development Jobs, Web Designer Job In USA, Web Developer Jobs Dublin, Web Developer California, Web Developer Calgary, Wellington Tech Jobs, Wireless System Engineer, Wix Designer Jobs, Work From Home Job Postings, Work From Home Software Testing Jobs, Working At Microsoft Store, ZOHO CRM Jobs, Indeed Computer Science Internship, Indeed Computer Science Internship, IT Works Jobs, IT Jobs Boston Ma

10 TOP 300+ ROLES IN IT ON INDEED (UK)

The digital tool for this chapter is
https://itjobsformula.com/indeedcouk/

IT Role Keyword   **URL**

3d animation London

https://www.indeed.co.uk/3d-Animation-jobs-in-London

3d artist jobs London

https://www.indeed.co.uk/3d-Artist-jobs-in-London

ABAP jobs London

https://www.indeed.co.uk/SAP-ABAP-Developer-jobs-in-London

Affiliate marketing jobs London

https://www.indeed.co.uk/Online-Affiliate-Marketing-jobs-in-London

Analyst jobs London

https://www.indeed.co.uk/Analyst-jobs-in-London

Analyst jobs Nottingham

https://www.indeed.co.uk/Analyst-jobs-in-Nottingham

Android developer Glasgow

https://www.indeed.co.uk/Android-Developer-jobs-in-Glasgow

Animation studios Manchester

https://www.indeed.co.uk/Animation-Studios-jobs-in-Manchester

App developer jobs London

https://www.indeed.co.uk/Mobile-Application-Developer-jobs-in-London

Beta testing jobs UK

https://www.indeed.co.uk/Beta-Tester-jobs-in-England

Big data Hadoop jobs in UK

https://www.indeed.co.uk/Hadoop-jobs-in-London

Brighton game studios

https://www.indeed.co.uk/Game-Studio-jobs-in-Brighton

Business analyst jobs Manchester

https://www.indeed.co.uk/Business-Analyst-jobs-in-Manchester

Business analyst jobs Newcastle upon Tyne

https://www.indeed.co.uk/Business-Analyst-jobs-in-Newcastle-upon-Tyne

Business analyst jobs north west

https://www.indeed.co.uk/Business-Analyst-jobs-in-North-West

Business analyst roles London

https://www.indeed.co.uk/Business-Analyst-jobs-in-London

Business continuity jobs London

https://www.indeed.co.uk/Business-Continuity-jobs-in-London

Business data analyst jobs London

https://www.indeed.co.uk/Business-Data-Analyst-jobs

Business development executive jobs London

https://www.indeed.co.uk/Business-Development-Executive-jobs-in-London

Business intelligence London

https://www.indeed.co.uk/Business-Intelligence-jobs-in-London

C programming jobs London

https://www.indeed.co.uk/C-Programmer-jobs-in-London

C++ developer jobs London

https://www.indeed.co.uk/C++-Developer-jobs-in-London

C++ finance jobs London

https://www.indeed.co.uk/C++-Developer-Finance-jobs-in-London

C++ jobs UK

https://www.indeed.co.uk/C++-jobs

Cad jobs north east

https://www.indeed.co.uk/CAD-jobs-in-North-East

Cad technician jobs Bath

https://www.indeed.co.uk/CAD-Technician-jobs-in-Bath

CCIE contract jobs UK

https://www.indeed.co.uk/Ccie-Ccie-Contract-jobs

Chief information officer jobs UK

https://www.indeed.co.uk/Chief-Information-Officer-jobs

Chief operating officer jobs London

https://www.indeed.co.uk/Chief-Operating-Officer-jobs-in-London

CISO jobs London

https://www.indeed.co.uk/Ciso-jobs-in-London

CISSP London jobs

https://www.indeed.co.uk/Cissp-jobs-in-London

Cobol CICS DB2 jobs UK

https://www.indeed.co.uk/Cobol-CICS-jobs-in-England

Cobol jobs UK

https://www.indeed.co.uk/Cobol-jobs

Cobol programming jobs UK

https://www.indeed.co.uk/Cobol-Developer-jobs

CompTIA Security+ jobs UK

https://www.indeed.co.uk/Comptia-jobs-in-England

Computer jobs in England

https://www.indeed.co.uk/Computer-jobs-in-England

Computer repair jobs Nottingham

https://www.indeed.co.uk/Computer-Repair-jobs-in-Nottingham

Computer science graduate jobs Manchester

https://www.indeed.co.uk/Computer-Science-Graduate-jobs-in-Manchester

Computer support jobs London

https://www.indeed.co.uk/Computer-Support-jobs-in-London

Computer vision UK

https://www.indeed.co.uk/Computer-Vision-Engineer-jobs-in-England

Content jobs Kent

https://www.indeed.co.uk/Content-jobs-in-Kent

Continuous improvement jobs Scotland

https://www.indeed.co.uk/Continuous-Improvement-Manager-jobs-in-Scotland

Copywriter London

https://www.indeed.co.uk/Copywriter-jobs-in-London

Crypto custodian jobs UK

https://www.indeed.co.uk/Crypto-Security-jobs

CTO roles London

https://www.indeed.co.uk/CTO-jobs-in-London

Cyber intelligence London

https://www.indeed.co.uk/Cyber-Intelligence-jobs-in-London

Cyber security apprenticeships Manchester

https://www.indeed.co.uk/Cyber-Security-Apprenticeship-jobs-in-Manchester

Cyber security jobs UK

https://www.indeed.co.uk/Cyber-Security-jobs

Data analysis jobs UK

https://www.indeed.co.uk/Data-Analyst-jobs

Data analyst internship London

https://www.indeed.co.uk/Data-Analyst-Intern-jobs-in-London

Data analyst jobs Edinburgh

https://www.indeed.co.uk/Data-Analyst-jobs-in-Edinburgh

Data analyst jobs London UK

https://www.indeed.co.uk/Data-Analyst-jobs-in-London

Data engineer jobs Scotland

https://www.indeed.co.uk/Data-Engineer-jobs-in-Scotland

Data entry jobs Swindon

https://www.indeed.co.uk/Data-Entry-jobs-in-Swindon

Data governance jobs London

https://www.indeed.co.uk/Data-Governance-jobs-in-London

Data protection jobs Cardiff

https://www.indeed.co.uk/Data-Protection-jobs-in-Cardiff

Data quality analyst jobs London

https://www.indeed.co.uk/Data-Quality-Analyst-jobs-in-London

Data science Belfast

https://www.indeed.co.uk/Data-Science-jobs-in-Belfast

Data science contract jobs London

https://www.indeed.co.uk/Data-Scientist-jobs-in-London

Data science jobs Nottingham

https://www.indeed.co.uk/Data-Scientist-jobs-in-Nottingham

Data scientist jobs Leeds

https://www.indeed.co.uk/Data-Scientist-jobs-in-Leeds

Data scientist jobs Wales

https://www.indeed.co.uk/Data-Scientist-jobs-in-Wales

Data strategy jobs London

https://www.indeed.co.uk/Data-Strategist-jobs-in-London

Dba contract jobs UK

https://www.indeed.co.uk/Oracle-DBA-Contract-jobs

Dba jobs London

https://www.indeed.co.uk/Database-Administrator-jobs-in-London

Delphi jobs UK

https://www.indeed.co.uk/Delphi-jobs

Desktop publishing jobs London

https://www.indeed.co.uk/Desktop-Publishing-jobs-in-London

Developer jobs Bristol

https://www.indeed.co.uk/Software-Developer-jobs-in-Bristol

Developer jobs London

https://www.indeed.co.uk/Software-Developer-jobs-in-London

DevOps engineer jobs London

https://www.indeed.co.uk/Devop-Engineer-jobs-in-Greater-London

Digital agency jobs Leeds

https://www.indeed.co.uk/Digital-Agency-jobs-in-Leeds

Digital analyst jobs London

https://www.indeed.co.uk/Digital-Analyst-jobs-in-London

Digital copywriter jobs London

https://www.indeed.co.uk/Digital-Copywriter-jobs-in-London

Digital director jobs London

https://www.indeed.co.uk/Digital-Director-jobs-in-London

Digital internships London

https://www.indeed.co.uk/Digital-Intern-jobs

Digital jobs Cardiff

https://www.indeed.co.uk/Digital-jobs-in-Cardiff

Digital jobs Glasgow

https://www.indeed.co.uk/Digital-jobs-in-Glasgow

Digital jobs Scotland

https://www.indeed.co.uk/Digital-jobs-in-Scotland

Digital manager jobs London

https://www.indeed.co.uk/Digital-Manager-jobs-in-London

Digital marketing director jobs London

https://www.indeed.co.uk/Digital-Marketing-Manager-jobs-in-London

Digital marketing Eastbourne

https://www.indeed.co.uk/Digital-Marketing-jobs-in-Eastbourne

Digital marketing internship London

https://www.indeed.co.uk/Digital-Marketing-Internship-jobs-in-London

Digital marketing internship UK

https://www.indeed.co.uk/Digital-Marketing-Internship-jobs

Digital marketing jobs Aberdeen

https://www.indeed.co.uk/Digital-Marketing-jobs-in-Aberdeen

Digital marketing jobs Cornwall

https://www.indeed.co.uk/Digital-Marketing-jobs-in-Cornwall

Digital marketing jobs London

https://www.indeed.co.uk/Digital-Marketing-jobs-in-London

Digital marketing jobs Scotland

https://www.indeed.co.uk/Digital-Marketing-jobs-in-Scotland

Digital marketing manager jobs London

https://www.indeed.co.uk/Digital-Marketing-Manager-jobs-in-London

Digital project manager London

https://www.indeed.co.uk/Digital-Project-Manager-jobs-in-London

Digital sales jobs London

https://www.indeed.co.uk/Digital-Sales-Executive-jobs-in-London

Distance jobs UK

https://www.indeed.co.uk/Online-Distance-jobs-in-England

Drupal jobs London

https://www.indeed.co.uk/Drupal-Developer-jobs-in-London

DV cleared network engineer

https://www.indeed.co.uk/Dv-Cleared-Network-Engineer-jobs

Ecommerce jobs Nottingham

https://www.indeed.co.uk/Ecommerce-jobs-in-Nottingham

Email marketing jobs UK

https://www.indeed.co.uk/Email-Marketing-jobs-in-London

Embedded jobs UK

https://www.indeed.co.uk/Embedded-Software-Engineer-jobs

Embedded software engineer jobs London

https://www.indeed.co.uk/Embedded-Software-Engineer-jobs-in-London

Entry level data analyst jobs London

https://www.indeed.co.uk/Entry-Level-Data-Analyst-jobs-in-London

Entry level programming jobs UK

https://www.indeed.co.uk/Entry-Level-Programmer-jobs-in-England

Entry level salesforce jobs UK

https://www.indeed.co.uk/Junior-Salesforce-jobs-in-London

Fibre optic jobs Scotland

https://www.indeed.co.uk/Fibre-Optics-jobs-in-Scotland

Freelance analyst jobs UK

https://www.indeed.co.uk/Freelance-Analyst-jobs

Freelance content writing jobs UK

https://www.indeed.co.uk/Freelance-Content-Writer-jobs

Freelance copywriting jobs UK

https://www.indeed.co.uk/Freelance-Copywriter-jobs

Freelance editing jobs UK

https://www.indeed.co.uk/Freelance-Editor-jobs

Freelance it jobs UK

https://www.indeed.co.uk/Freelance-IT-jobs

Freelance SEO jobs UK

https://www.indeed.co.uk/Freelance-SEO-jobs

Front end developer Glasgow

https://www.indeed.co.uk/Front-End-Developer-jobs-in-Glasgow

Front end developer internship London

https://www.indeed.co.uk/Front-End-Developer-Intern-jobs

Front end developer remote jobs UK

https://www.indeed.co.uk/Remote-Developer-jobs

Front end jobs in London

https://www.indeed.co.uk/Front-End-Developer-jobs-in-London

Front end web developer jobs Manchester

https://www.indeed.co.uk/Front-End-Developer-jobs-in-Manchester

Front end web developer London

https://www.indeed.co.uk/Front-End-Web-Developer-jobs-in-London

Full stack developer London

https://www.indeed.co.uk/Full-Stack-Developer-jobs-in-London

Game designer jobs UK

https://www.indeed.co.uk/Video-Game-Designer-jobs

Game developer jobs London

https://www.indeed.co.uk/Game-Programmer-jobs-in-London

Game developer jobs UK

https://www.indeed.co.uk/Video-Game-Developer-jobs

Game jobs Bristol

https://www.indeed.co.uk/Games-jobs-in-Bristol

Game writer jobs London

https://www.indeed.co.uk/Game-Writer-jobs-in-London

GIS analyst jobs London

https://www.indeed.co.uk/GIS-Analyst-jobs-in-London

GIS jobs Glasgow

https://www.indeed.co.uk/GIS-jobs-in-Glasgow

GIS jobs Scotland UK

https://www.indeed.co.uk/GIS-jobs-in-Scotland

GIS jobs UK

https://www.indeed.co.uk/GIS-jobs

GIS specialist jobs London

https://www.indeed.co.uk/GIS-Specialist-jobs-in-London

Graduate data scientist jobs London

https://www.indeed.co.uk/Data-Scientist-jobs

Graduate it support analyst

https://www.indeed.co.uk/Graduate-IT-Support-Analyst-jobs

Graphic design jobs Bedfordshire

https://www.indeed.co.uk/Graphic-Designer-jobs-in-Bedfordshire

Graphic design jobs Bournemouth

https://www.indeed.co.uk/Graphic-Designer-jobs-in-Bournemouth

Graphic design jobs Buckinghamshire

https://www.indeed.co.uk/Graphic-Designer-jobs-in-Buckinghamshire

Graphic design jobs Cheshire

https://www.indeed.co.uk/Graphic-Designer-jobs-in-Cheshire

Graphic design jobs Essex

https://www.indeed.co.uk/Graphic-Designer-jobs-in-Essex

Graphic design jobs from home UK

https://www.indeed.co.uk/Graphic-Design-Home-Based-jobs

Graphic design jobs London England

https://www.indeed.co.uk/Graphic-Designer-jobs-in-London

Graphic design jobs Maidstone

https://www.indeed.co.uk/Graphic-Designer-jobs-in-Maidstone

Graphic design jobs Scotland

https://www.indeed.co.uk/Graphic-Designer-jobs-in-Scotland

Graphic design jobs Warrington

https://www.indeed.co.uk/Graphic-Designer-jobs-in-Warrington

Graphic design manager jobs London

https://www.indeed.co.uk/Graphic-Design-Manager-jobs

Graphic designer Herts

https://www.indeed.co.uk/Graphic-Designer-jobs-in-Hertfordshire

Graphic designer Poole

https://www.indeed.co.uk/Graphic-Designer-jobs-in-Poole

Hadoop administrator jobs in UK

https://www.indeed.co.uk/Hadoop-Administrator-jobs

Head of IT Birmingham

https://www.indeed.co.uk/Head-of-IT-jobs-in-Birmingham

Helpdesk support jobs London

https://www.indeed.co.uk/Helpdesk-jobs-in-London

Hull graphic design jobs

https://www.indeed.co.uk/Graphic-Design-jobs-in-Kingston-upon-Hull

Hyperion planning jobs in London

https://www.indeed.co.uk/Oracle-Hyperion-Planning-jobs

IBM jobs Southampton

https://www.indeed.co.uk/IBM-jobs-in-Southampton

IBM Leicester jobs

https://www.indeed.co.uk/IBM-jobs-in-Leicester

ICT apprenticeships London

https://www.indeed.co.uk/Ict-Apprenticeship-jobs-in-London

ICT apprenticeships near me

https://www.indeed.co.uk/Ict-Apprenticeship-jobs

ICT police jobs

https://www.indeed.co.uk/Ict-Police-jobs

Infojobs co UK

https://www.indeed.co.uk/Info-jobs

Informatica contract jobs in London

https://www.indeed.co.uk/Informatica-Contract-jobs

Information security jobs Bristol

https://www.indeed.co.uk/Information-Security-jobs-in-Bristol

Information security jobs Newcastle upon Tyne

https://www.indeed.co.uk/Information-Security-jobs-in-Newcastle-upon-Tyne

IT administrator jobs London

https://www.indeed.co.uk/IT-Administrator-jobs-in-London

IT apprenticeships Kent

https://www.indeed.co.uk/IT-Apprenticeships-jobs-in-Kent

IT apprenticeships Peterborough

https://www.indeed.co.uk/IT-Apprenticeships-jobs-in-Peterborough

IT apprenticeships Southampton

https://www.indeed.co.uk/IT-Apprenticeships-jobs-in-Southampton

IT auditor jobs UK

https://www.indeed.co.uk/IT-Auditor-jobs

IT consultant Manchester

https://www.indeed.co.uk/IT-Consultant-jobs-in-Manchester

IT contracts UK

https://www.indeed.co.uk/UK-IT-Contracts-jobs

IT director jobs East Midlands

https://www.indeed.co.uk/IT-Director-jobs-in-East-Midlands-Airport

IT director jobs UK

https://www.indeed.co.uk/IT-Director-jobs

IT graduate schemes London

https://www.indeed.co.uk/IT-Graduate-jobs-in-London

IT infrastructure jobs London

https://www.indeed.co.uk/IT-Infrastructure-jobs-in-London

IT jobs Dorset

https://www.indeed.co.uk/IT-jobs-in-Dorset

IT jobs Fife

https://www.indeed.co.uk/IT-jobs-in-Fife

IT jobs Glasgow

https://www.indeed.co.uk/IT-jobs-in-Glasgow

IT jobs Guildford

https://www.indeed.co.uk/IT-jobs-in-Guildford

IT jobs in Coventry and Warwickshire

https://www.indeed.co.uk/IT-jobs-in-Coventry

IT jobs in England

https://www.indeed.co.uk/IT-jobs

IT jobs Leeds

https://www.indeed.co.uk/IT-jobs-in-Leeds

IT jobs Leicester

https://www.indeed.co.uk/IT-jobs-in-Leicester

IT jobs Nottinghamshire

https://www.indeed.co.uk/IT-jobs-in-Nottingham

IT jobs Scotland

https://www.indeed.co.uk/IT-jobs-in-Scotland

IT jobs Slough

https://www.indeed.co.uk/IT-jobs-in-Slough

IT jobs Stevenage

https://www.indeed.co.uk/IT-jobs-in-Stevenage

IT jobs Sunderland

https://www.indeed.co.uk/IT-jobs-in-Sunderland

IT jobs UK

https://www.indeed.co.uk/IT-jobs

IT manager jobs Brighton

https://www.indeed.co.uk/IT-Manager-jobs-in-Brighton

IT manager jobs Ipswich

https://www.indeed.co.uk/IT-Manager-jobs-in-Ipswich

IT manager jobs Leeds

https://www.indeed.co.uk/IT-Manager-jobs-in-Leeds

IT manager jobs Milton Keynes

https://www.indeed.co.uk/IT-Manager-jobs-in-Milton-Keynes

IT manager jobs Swindon

https://www.indeed.co.uk/IT-Manager-jobs-in-Swindon

IT manager Manchester

https://www.indeed.co.uk/IT-Manager-jobs-in-Manchester

IT security London jobs

https://www.indeed.co.uk/Cyber-Security-jobs-in-London

IT support analyst jobs London

https://www.indeed.co.uk/IT-Support-Analyst-jobs-in-London

IT support technician jobs in Liverpool

https://www.indeed.co.uk/IT-Technician-jobs-in-Liverpool

IT support technician jobs UK

https://www.indeed.co.uk/IT-Support-Technician-jobs

IT teaching jobs UK

https://www.indeed.co.uk/IT-Teacher-jobs

IT technician jobs Manchester

https://www.indeed.co.uk/IT-Support-Technician-jobs-in-Manchester

IT technician London

https://www.indeed.co.uk/IT-Technician-jobs-in-London

IT trainer jobs Bristol

https://www.indeed.co.uk/IT-Trainer-jobs-in-Bristol

IT trainer jobs UK

https://www.indeed.co.uk/IT-Trainer-jobs

Java developer jobs London UK

https://www.indeed.co.uk/Java-Developer-jobs-in-London

Java graduate jobs London

https://www.indeed.co.uk/Graduate-Java-Developer-jobs-in-London

Java Spring jobs London

https://www.indeed.co.uk/Java-Spring-Framework-jobs-in-London

JavaScript developer jobs London

https://www.indeed.co.uk/Javascript-Developer-jobs-in-London

JavaScript jobs London

https://www.indeed.co.uk/Javascript-jobs-in-London

Junior analyst jobs London

https://www.indeed.co.uk/Junior-Analyst-jobs-in-London

Junior game developer jobs UK

https://www.indeed.co.uk/Junior-Game-Developer-jobs

Junior graphic design jobs Bristol

https://www.indeed.co.uk/Junior-Designer-jobs-in-Bristol

Junior graphic design jobs UK

https://www.indeed.co.uk/Junior-Graphic-Designer-jobs

Junior Java developer jobs UK

https://www.indeed.co.uk/Junior-Java-Developer-jobs

Junior JavaScript developer jobs London

https://www.indeed.co.uk/Junior-Javascript-Developer-jobs-in-London

Junior network engineer London

https://www.indeed.co.uk/Junior-Network-Engineer-jobs-in-London

Junior Oracle DBA jobs in UK

https://www.indeed.co.uk/Junior-Oracle-DBA-jobs-in-England

Junior programmer jobs London

https://www.indeed.co.uk/Junior-Programmer-jobs-in-London

Junior SAP jobs UK

https://www.indeed.co.uk/Junior-SAP-Consultant-jobs

Junior software developer Edinburgh

https://www.indeed.co.uk/Junior-Software-Developer-jobs-in-Edinburgh

Junior SQL jobs London

https://www.indeed.co.uk/Junior-SQL-jobs-in-London

Junior web designer London

https://www.indeed.co.uk/Junior-Web-Designer-jobs-in-London

Junior web developer jobs Glasgow

https://www.indeed.co.uk/Junior-Web-Developer-jobs-in-Glasgow

Junior web developer jobs UK

https://www.indeed.co.uk/Junior-Web-Developer-jobs

Lean Six Sigma jobs UK

https://www.indeed.co.uk/Lean-Six-Sigma-jobs

Linux admin jobs in UK

https://www.indeed.co.uk/Linux-System-Administrator-jobs-in-London

Linux engineer jobs London

https://www.indeed.co.uk/Linux-Engineer-jobs-in-London

Mac jobs Leeds

https://www.indeed.co.uk/Mac-jobs-in-Leeds

Magento jobs London

https://www.indeed.co.uk/Magento-jobs-in-London

Mainframe job openings in UK

https://www.indeed.co.uk/IBM-Mainframe-jobs-in-England

Marketing automation jobs UK

https://www.indeed.co.uk/Marketing-Automation-jobs

Master data jobs London

https://www.indeed.co.uk/Master-Data-jobs-in-London

Microsoft CRM jobs UK

https://www.indeed.co.uk/Dynamics-Crm-jobs

Mobile developer jobs London

https://www.indeed.co.uk/Mobile-Application-Developer-jobs-in-London

MS jobs UK

https://www.indeed.co.uk/Ms-jobs

Network engineer jobs Glasgow

https://www.indeed.co.uk/Network-Engineer-jobs-in-Glasgow

Network engineer jobs Ipswich

https://www.indeed.co.uk/Network-Engineer-jobs-in-Ipswich

Network security jobs Edinburgh

https://www.indeed.co.uk/Cyber-Security-jobs-in-Edinburgh

Newcastle web design jobs

https://www.indeed.co.uk/Web-Designer-jobs-in-Newcastle-upon-Tyne

NHS IT contract

https://www.indeed.co.uk/Nhs-IT-Contract-jobs

Online paid jobs UK

https://www.indeed.co.uk/Online-Paid-jobs

Operations manager jobs Aberdeen

https://www.indeed.co.uk/Operations-Manager-jobs-in-Aberdeen

Oracle BPM jobs UK

https://www.indeed.co.uk/Oracle-Bpm-jobs

Oracle Linlithgow jobs

https://www.indeed.co.uk/Oracle-jobs-in-Linlithgow

Pega developer jobs in UK

https://www.indeed.co.uk/Pega-Developer-jobs

Photo editing jobs UK

https://www.indeed.co.uk/Photo-Editor-jobs

PHP jobs Manchester

https://www.indeed.co.uk/PHP-Developer-jobs-in-Manchester

Presentation designer jobs London

https://www.indeed.co.uk/Powerpoint-Presentation-Designer-jobs-in-London

Process engineer jobs UK

https://www.indeed.co.uk/Process-Engineer-jobs

Product developer jobs London

https://www.indeed.co.uk/Product-Developer-jobs-in-London

Programming jobs Belfast

https://www.indeed.co.uk/Computer-Programming-jobs-in-Belfast

Programming jobs from home UK

https://www.indeed.co.uk/Home-Based-Programmer-jobs-in-England

Project analyst jobs London

https://www.indeed.co.uk/Project-Analyst-jobs-in-London

Publishing design jobs London

https://www.indeed.co.uk/Publishing-Designer-jobs-in-London

Python jobs UK

https://www.indeed.co.uk/Python-jobs

Python programming jobs UK

https://www.indeed.co.uk/Python-Developer-jobs-in-London

QA game tester jobs UK

https://www.indeed.co.uk/QA-Games-Tester-jobs

Quantitative analyst UK

https://www.indeed.co.uk/Quantitative-Analyst-jobs

R programming jobs UK

https://www.indeed.co.uk/R-Programmer-jobs

Remote research jobs UK

https://www.indeed.co.uk/Remote-Researcher-jobs

Remote video editing jobs UK

https://www.indeed.co.uk/Freelance-Video-Editor-jobs

Research analyst London

https://www.indeed.co.uk/Research-Analyst-jobs

Ruby jobs UK

https://www.indeed.co.uk/Ruby-Rail-Developer-jobs-in-London

Salesforce developer jobs London

https://www.indeed.co.uk/Salesforce-Developer-jobs-in-London

Salesforce jobs Leeds

https://www.indeed.co.uk/Salesforce-jobs-in-Leeds

SAP ABAP jobs in London UK

https://www.indeed.co.uk/SAP-ABAP-jobs-in-London

SAP APO jobs in UK

https://www.indeed.co.uk/SAP-Apo-jobs

SAP business analyst jobs in London

https://www.indeed.co.uk/SAP-Business-Analyst-jobs-in-London

SAP business analyst jobs UK

https://www.indeed.co.uk/SAP-Business-Analyst-jobs

SAP data migration jobs in UK

https://www.indeed.co.uk/SAP-Data-Migration-jobs

SAP Fico contract jobs London

https://www.indeed.co.uk/SAP-Fico-Contract-jobs

SAP jobs Aberdeen

https://www.indeed.co.uk/SAP-jobs-in-Aberdeen

SAP jobs Bristol

https://www.indeed.co.uk/SAP-jobs-in-Bristol

SAP jobs London

https://www.indeed.co.uk/SAP-jobs-in-London

SAP security jobs in London

https://www.indeed.co.uk/SAP-Security-jobs-in-London

SAS jobs Edinburgh

https://www.indeed.co.uk/SAS-jobs-in-Edinburgh

SAS jobs London

https://www.indeed.co.uk/SAS-jobs-in-London

SAS programmer UK

https://www.indeed.co.uk/SAS-Programmer-jobs

Scientific computing jobs UK

https://www.indeed.co.uk/Scientific-Computing-jobs

Scrum master jobs London

https://www.indeed.co.uk/Scrum-Master-jobs-in-London

SEO jobs Leeds

https://www.indeed.co.uk/SEO-jobs-in-Leeds

SEO manager London

https://www.indeed.co.uk/SEO-Manager-jobs-in-London

SEO marketing jobs Manchester

https://www.indeed.co.uk/SEO-jobs-in-Manchester

SEO writing jobs UK

https://www.indeed.co.uk/SEO-Writer-jobs

SharePoint jobs Manchester

https://www.indeed.co.uk/Sharepoint-jobs-in-Manchester

SharePoint London jobs

https://www.indeed.co.uk/Microsoft-Sharepoint-jobs-in-London

Siemens Rugby

https://www.indeed.co.uk/Siemens-jobs-in-Rugby

Six Sigma black belt jobs London

https://www.indeed.co.uk/Six-Sigma-Black-Belt-jobs

Sketchup jobs London

https://www.indeed.co.uk/Sketchup-jobs-in-London

Social marketing jobs London

https://www.indeed.co.uk/Social-Marketing-jobs-in-London

Social media consultant jobs London

https://www.indeed.co.uk/Social-Media-Consultant-jobs-in-London

Social media jobs Brighton

https://www.indeed.co.uk/Social-Media-jobs-in-Brighton

Social media jobs Leeds

https://www.indeed.co.uk/Social-Media-jobs-in-Leeds

Social media jobs London

https://www.indeed.co.uk/Social-Media-jobs

Social media jobs Manchester

https://www.indeed.co.uk/Social-Media-jobs-in-Manchester

Software developer apprenticeship Birmingham

https://www.indeed.co.uk/Software-Apprentice-jobs-in-Birmingham

Software developer Glasgow

https://www.indeed.co.uk/Software-Developer-jobs-in-Glasgow

Software development internship UK

https://www.indeed.co.uk/Software-Development-Internship-jobs

Software development jobs northern Ireland

https://www.indeed.co.uk/Software-Developer-jobs-in-Northern-Ireland

Software engineering jobs in England

https://www.indeed.co.uk/Software-Engineer-jobs

Software jobs Aberdeen

https://www.indeed.co.uk/Software-Developer-jobs-in-Aberdeen

Software testing contract jobs in London

https://www.indeed.co.uk/Software-Tester-Contract-jobs-in-London

Software testing jobs in London UK

https://www.indeed.co.uk/Software-Testing-jobs-in-London

SQL developer jobs UK

https://www.indeed.co.uk/SQL-Developer-jobs-in-London

Sysadmin jobs London

https://www.indeed.co.uk/System-Administrator-jobs-in-London

Systems analyst jobs UK

https://www.indeed.co.uk/Systems-Analyst-jobs

Tableau London jobs

https://www.indeed.co.uk/Tableau-jobs-in-London

Tech internships London

https://www.indeed.co.uk/Technology-Internship-jobs-in-London

Tech support jobs London

https://www.indeed.co.uk/Technical-Support-jobs-in-London

Technical author jobs UK

https://www.indeed.co.uk/Technical-Author-jobs

Technical business analyst jobs London

https://www.indeed.co.uk/Technical-Business-Analyst-jobs-in-London

Technical writer jobs UK

https://www.indeed.co.uk/Technical-Writer-jobs

Test analyst jobs Glasgow

https://www.indeed.co.uk/Test-Analyst-jobs-in-Glasgow

Test analyst jobs Leads

https://www.indeed.co.uk/Test-Analyst-jobs-in-Leeds

Trainee IT technician London

https://www.indeed.co.uk/Trainee-IT-Technician-jobs-in-London

UAT jobs London

https://www.indeed.co.uk/Uat-jobs-in-London

UI UX designer jobs London

https://www.indeed.co.uk/Ui-Ux-Designer-jobs-in-London

Unity jobs London

https://www.indeed.co.uk/Unity3d-jobs-in-London

UX design internship London

https://www.indeed.co.uk/Ux-Intern-jobs-in-London

UX designer jobs LONDON

https://www.indeed.co.uk/User-Experience-Designer-jobs-in-London

UX jobs Bristol

https://www.indeed.co.uk/Ux-jobs-in-Bristol

UX jobs London

https://www.indeed.co.uk/Ux-jobs-in-London

VFX internship London

https://www.indeed.co.uk/Vfx-jobs-in-London

Video game writer jobs UK

https://www.indeed.co.uk/Game-Writer-jobs

Virtual administrative assistant UK

https://www.indeed.co.uk/Virtual-Assistant-jobs

Virtual assistant jobs London

https://www.indeed.co.uk/Virtual-Assistant-jobs-in-London

Visual effects jobs London

https://www.indeed.co.uk/Visual-Effects-jobs-in-London

Vue JS jobs London

https://www.indeed.co.uk/Vue-jobs-in-London

Web design jobs Bournemouth

https://www.indeed.co.uk/Web-Design-jobs-in-Bournemouth

Web design jobs Nottingham

https://www.indeed.co.uk/Web-Designer-jobs-in-Nottingham

Web developer Cheltenham

https://www.indeed.co.uk/Web-Developer-jobs-in-Cheltenham

Web developer Edinburgh

https://www.indeed.co.uk/Web-Developer-jobs-in-Edinburgh

Web developer Exeter

https://www.indeed.co.uk/Web-Developer-jobs-in-Exeter

Web developer internship UK

https://www.indeed.co.uk/Web-Developer-Internship-jobs

Web developer jobs Birmingham UK

https://www.indeed.co.uk/Web-Developer-jobs-in-Birmingham

Web developer jobs Glasgow

https://www.indeed.co.uk/Web-Developer-jobs-in-Glasgow

Web developer jobs Liverpool

https://www.indeed.co.uk/Web-Developer-jobs-in-Liverpool

Web developer Watford

https://www.indeed.co.uk/Web-Developer-jobs-in-Watford

Work from home jobs London data entry

https://www.indeed.co.uk/Data-Entry-At-Home-jobs-in-London

Xbox jobs London

https://www.indeed.co.uk/Microsoft-Xbox-jobs-in-London

Yahoo jobs London UK

https://www.indeed.co.uk/Yahoo-jobs-in-London

11 INDEED (UK) IT ROLES BY POPULARITY

This shows IT Roles by Internet traffic in descending order. Which IT Role phrases are the most popular?

IT jobs UK, beta testing jobs UK, business data analyst jobs London, business intelligence London, CompTIA security+ jobs UK, content jobs Kent, cyber intelligence London, data protection jobs Cardiff, data scientist jobs wales, developer jobs London, digital jobs Glasgow, digital marketing jobs Cornwall, fibre optic jobs Scotland, graphic design jobs Buckinghamshire, ICT apprenticeships near me, IT contracts UK, IT jobs Glasgow, IT manager jobs Ipswich, IT manager jobs Swindon, Java graduate jobs London, Java spring jobs London, JavaScript developer jobs London, JavaScript jobs London, junior network engineer London, Newcastle web design jobs, Pega developer jobs in UK, process engineer jobs UK, programming jobs Belfast, python jobs UK, QA game tester jobs UK, Salesforce jobs Leeds, SAP ABAP jobs in London UK, SharePoint jobs Manchester, social media jobs Leeds, social media jobs London, software jobs Aberdeen, software testing jobs in London UK, Tableau London jobs, Unity jobs London, Xbox jobs London, 3d animation London, ABAP jobs London, business analyst jobs Newcastle upon Tyne, business analyst roles London, C++ finance jobs London, CCIE contract jobs UK, Cobol CICS DB2 jobs UK, computer repair jobs Nottingham, cyber security jobs UK, data governance jobs London, data quality analyst jobs London, data science jobs Nottingham, DBA jobs London, Delphi jobs UK, desktop publishing jobs London, developer jobs Bristol, digital agency jobs Leeds, digital jobs Scotland, digital marketing Eastbourne, digital marketing internship UK, digital marketing jobs Aberdeen, digital marketing jobs London, digital marketing manager jobs London, digital project manager London, digital sales jobs London, Drupal jobs London, embedded jobs UK, freelance content writing jobs UK, freelance copywriting jobs UK, freelance IT jobs UK, front end jobs in London, game developer jobs London, GIS jobs Scotland UK, GIS jobs

UK, graduate IT support analyst, graphic design jobs Bedfordshire, graphic design jobs Bournemouth, graphic design jobs Essex, graphic design manager jobs London, Hadoop administrator jobs in UK, IBM Leicester jobs, ICT apprenticeships London, informatica contract jobs in London, IT apprenticeships Southampton, IT director jobs east midlands, IT director jobs UK, IT graduate schemes London, IT jobs Guildford, IT jobs in England, IT jobs Leeds, IT jobs Nottinghamshire, IT jobs Slough, IT manager jobs Leeds, IT technician London, IT trainer jobs UK, junior graphic design jobs Bristol, junior software developer Edinburgh, junior web developer jobs UK, Linux admin jobs in UK, master data jobs London, network engineer jobs Ipswich, Oracle Linlithgow jobs, PHP jobs Manchester, product developer jobs London, project analyst jobs London, publishing design jobs London, Ruby jobs UK, SAP Fico contract jobs London, SAP jobs Aberdeen, SAP jobs London, SAP security jobs in London, scientific computing jobs UK, scrum master jobs London, SEO manager London, SEO writing jobs UK, Siemens Rugby, social media jobs Brighton, social media jobs Manchester, software developer apprenticeship Birmingham, software developer Glasgow, software development internship UK, software development jobs Northern Ireland, SQL developer jobs UK, tech internships London, technical author jobs UK, test analyst jobs Glasgow, trainee IT technician London, UAT jobs London, UX jobs Bristol, UX jobs London, VFX internship London, video game writer jobs UK, virtual administrative assistant UK, virtual assistant jobs London, visual effects jobs London, web developer Edinburgh, web developer jobs Birmingham UK, web developer jobs Glasgow, work from home jobs London data entry, Android developer Glasgow, app developer jobs London, C programming jobs London, C++ developer jobs London, CAD jobs north east, CAD technician jobs Bath, Chief Information Officer jobs UK, copywriter London, CTO roles London, cyber security apprenticeships Manchester, data analysis jobs UK, data analyst internship London, data analyst jobs London UK, data engineer jobs Scotland, data entry jobs Swindon, data science Belfast, data science contract jobs London, DBA contract jobs UK, digital analyst jobs London, digital director jobs London, digital manager jobs London, digital marketing director jobs London, digital marketing internship London, digital marketing jobs Scotland, dv cleared network engineer, ecommerce jobs Nottingham, email marketing jobs UK, entry level programming jobs UK, entry level Salesforce jobs UK, freelance analyst jobs UK, front end developer Glasgow, front end developer internship London, full stack developer London, GIS specialist jobs London, graphic design jobs Warrington, graphic designer Poole, Hull graphic design jobs, IBM jobs Southampton, infojobs co UK, IT infrastructure jobs London, IT jobs Fife, IT jobs Leicester, IT manager jobs Brighton, IT support analyst jobs London, IT technician jobs Manchester, junior game developer jobs UK, junior Java developer jobs UK, junior programmer jobs London, junior SAP jobs UK, junior web developer jobs Glasgow, lean Six Sigma jobs UK, Linux engineer jobs London, mainframe job openings in UK, marketing automation jobs UK, network security jobs Edinburgh, NHS IT contract, presentation designer jobs London, programming jobs from home UK, SAP APO jobs in UK, SAP data migration jobs in UK, SAS programmer UK, SEO jobs Leeds, SEO marketing jobs Manchester, Six Sigma black belt jobs London, social marketing jobs London, social media consultant jobs London, software engineering jobs in England, software testing contract jobs in London, tech support jobs London, test analyst jobs Leeds, UI UX designer jobs London, Vue JS jobs London, web developer Cheltenham, web developer Exeter, web developer Watford, 3d artist jobs London, affiliate marketing jobs London, analyst jobs Nottingham, animation studios Manchester, big data Hadoop jobs in UK, Brighton game studios, business analyst jobs Manchester, business analyst jobs north west, business continuity jobs London, business development executive jobs London, C++ jobs UK, Chief Operating Officer jobs London, CISO jobs London, CISSP London jobs, Cobol jobs UK, Cobol programming jobs UK, computer jobs in England, computer science graduate jobs Manchester, computer support jobs London, computer vision UK, continuous improvement jobs Scotland, crypto custodian jobs UK, data scientist jobs Leeds, data strategy jobs London, DevOps engineer jobs London, digital copywriter jobs London, digital internships London, digital jobs Cardiff, distance jobs UK, embedded software engineer jobs London, freelance editing jobs UK, freelance SEO jobs UK, front end developer remote jobs UK, front end web developer jobs Manchester, front end web developer London, game designer jobs UK, game developer jobs UK, game jobs Bristol, game writer jobs London, GIS jobs Glasgow, graduate data scientist jobs London, graphic design jobs Cheshire, graphic design jobs from home UK, graphic design jobs London England, graphic design jobs Maidstone, graphic design jobs Scotland, graphic designer Herts, head of IT Birmingham, helpdesk support jobs London, Hyperion planning jobs in London, ICT police jobs, information security jobs Bristol, information security jobs Newcastle upon Tyne, IT administrator jobs London, IT apprenticeships Kent, IT apprenticeships Peterborough, IT auditor jobs UK, IT consultant Manchester, IT jobs Dorset, IT jobs in Coventry and Warwickshire, IT jobs Scotland, IT jobs Stevenage, IT jobs Sunderland, IT manager jobs Milton Keynes, IT manager Manchester, IT security London jobs, IT support technician jobs in Liverpool, IT teaching jobs UK, IT trainer jobs Bristol, Java developer jobs London UK, junior graphic design jobs UK, junior JavaScript developer jobs London, junior Oracle DBA jobs in UK, junior SQL jobs London, junior web designer London, mac jobs Leeds, Magneto jobs London, Microsoft CRM jobs UK, mobile developer jobs London, MS jobs UK, network engineer jobs Glasgow, online paid jobs UK, operations manager jobs Aberdeen, Oracle BPM jobs UK, photo editing jobs UK, Python programming jobs UK, quantitative analyst UK, R programming jobs UK, remote research jobs UK, remote video editing jobs UK, research analyst London, Salesforce developer jobs London, SAP business analyst jobs in London, SAP business analyst jobs UK, SAP jobs Bristol, SAS jobs Edinburgh, SAS jobs London, SharePoint London jobs, SketchUp jobs London, sysadmin jobs London, systems analyst jobs UK, technical business analyst jobs London, technical writer jobs UK, UX design internship London, UX designer jobs London, web design jobs Bournemouth, web design jobs Nottingham, web developer internship UK, web developer jobs Liverpool, yahoo jobs London UK, analyst jobs London, data analyst jobs Edinburgh, entry level data analyst jobs London, GIS analyst jobs London, IT support technician jobs UK, junior analyst jobs London

12 TOP 200 ROLES IN IT ON ZIP RECRUITER (USA)

The digital tool for this chapter is
https://itjobsformula.com/ziprecruiter/

IT Role Keyword   **URL**

Comcast jobs

https://www.ziprecruiter.com/c/Comcast/Jobs

3d modelling jobs

https://www.ziprecruiter.com/Jobs/3D-Modeler

Active directory administrator

https://www.ziprecruiter.com/Jobs/Active-Directory-Administrator

Game tester jobs at home

https://www.ziprecruiter.com/Jobs/At-Home-Video-Game-Tester

Video game tester from home

https://www.ziprecruiter.com/Jobs/At-Home-Video-Game-Tester

Audio engineering jobs

https://www.ziprecruiter.com/Jobs/Audio-Engineer

Blockchain jobs

https://www.ziprecruiter.com/Jobs/Blockchain

Business analyst jobs

https://www.ziprecruiter.com/Jobs/Business-Analyst

Business systems analyst

https://www.ziprecruiter.com/Jobs/Business-Systems-Analyst

Ciso jobs

https://www.ziprecruiter.com/Jobs/CISO

CompTIA a+ jobs

https://www.ziprecruiter.com/Jobs/Comptia-A

Computer consultant

https://www.ziprecruiter.com/Jobs/Computer-Consultant

Computer engineering internships

https://www.ziprecruiter.com/Jobs/Computer-Engineer-Intern

Computer forensics jobs

https://www.ziprecruiter.com/Jobs/Computer-Forensics-Analyst

Network security jobs

https://www.ziprecruiter.com/Jobs/Computer-Networking-Security

Computer coding jobs from home

https://www.ziprecruiter.com/Jobs/Computer-Programmer-Work-From-Home

Computer support specialist jobs

https://www.ziprecruiter.com/Jobs/Computer-Support-Specialist

Computer technician jobs

https://www.ziprecruiter.com/Jobs/Computer-Technician

Copywriter jobs

https://www.ziprecruiter.com/Jobs/Copywriter

Intelligence analyst jobs

https://www.ziprecruiter.com/Jobs/Criminal-Intelligence-Analyst

Cyber security internships

https://www.ziprecruiter.com/Jobs/Cybersecurity-Internship

Data analyst jobs

https://www.ziprecruiter.com/Jobs/Data-Analyst

Data entry jobs

https://www.ziprecruiter.com/Jobs/Data-Entry

Excel jobs

https://www.ziprecruiter.com/Jobs/Data-Entry-Excel

Desktop support jobs

https://www.ziprecruiter.com/Jobs/Desktop-Support

DevOps jobs

https://www.ziprecruiter.com/Jobs/Devops

Animation jobs

https://www.ziprecruiter.com/Jobs/Digital-Animation

Digital marketing internship

https://www.ziprecruiter.com/Jobs/Digital-Marketing-Intern

Drone pilot jobs

https://www.ziprecruiter.com/Jobs/Drone-Pilot

Ecommerce jobs

https://www.ziprecruiter.com/Jobs/Ecommerce

Entry level business analyst jobs

https://www.ziprecruiter.com/Jobs/Entry-Level-Business-Analyst

Entry level coding jobs

https://www.ziprecruiter.com/Jobs/Entry-Level-Coding

Computer coding jobs

https://www.ziprecruiter.com/Jobs/Entry-Level-Computer-Programming

Entry level computer science jobs

https://www.ziprecruiter.com/Jobs/Entry-Level-Computer-Science

Entry level computer science jobs

https://www.ziprecruiter.com/Jobs/Entry-Level-Computer-Scientist

Cyber security jobs

https://www.ziprecruiter.com/Jobs/Entry-Level-Cyber-Security

Entry level cyber security jobs

https://www.ziprecruiter.com/Jobs/Entry-Level-Cyber-Security-Analyst

Entry level data analyst jobs

https://www.ziprecruiter.com/Jobs/Entry-Level-Data-Analyst

Entry level financial analyst

https://www.ziprecruiter.com/Jobs/Entry-Level-Financial-Analyst

Entry level help desk

https://www.ziprecruiter.com/Jobs/Entry-Level-Help-Desk-Analyst

MIS jobs

https://www.ziprecruiter.com/Jobs/Entry-Level-MIS

Entry level Python jobs

https://www.ziprecruiter.com/Jobs/Entry-Level-Python-Developer

Python developer jobs

https://www.ziprecruiter.com/Jobs/Entry-Level-Python-Developer

Salesforce entry level jobs

https://www.ziprecruiter.com/Jobs/Entry-Level-Salesforce-Administrator

Entry level software engineer

https://www.ziprecruiter.com/Jobs/Entry-Level-Software-Engineer

Entry level technical writer jobs

https://www.ziprecruiter.com/Jobs/Entry-Level-Technical-Writer

Virtual assistant jobs for beginners

https://www.ziprecruiter.com/Jobs/Entry-Level-Virtual-Assistant

Entry level work from home jobs

https://www.ziprecruiter.com/Jobs/Entry-Level-Work-From-Home

Epic careers

https://www.ziprecruiter.com/Jobs/Epic

Esports jobs

https://www.ziprecruiter.com/Jobs/Esports

Telework jobs

https://www.ziprecruiter.com/Jobs/Federal-Telework

Field service technician

https://www.ziprecruiter.com/Jobs/Field-Service-Technician

Flexible jobs

https://www.ziprecruiter.com/Jobs/Flexible-Virtual

Work from home flexible hours

https://www.ziprecruiter.com/Jobs/Flexible-Work-From-Home

Freelance computer programmer

https://www.ziprecruiter.com/Jobs/Freelance-Computer-Programmer

Freelance content writer

https://www.ziprecruiter.com/Jobs/Freelance-Content-Writer

Freelance graphic designer

https://www.ziprecruiter.com/Jobs/Freelance-Graphic-Designer

Freelance videographer

https://www.ziprecruiter.com/Jobs/Freelance-Videographer

Freelance web designer

https://www.ziprecruiter.com/Jobs/Freelance-Web-Designer

Freelance web developer

https://www.ziprecruiter.com/Jobs/Freelance-Web-Developer

Front end specialist

https://www.ziprecruiter.com/Jobs/Front-End-Specialist

Game design jobs

https://www.ziprecruiter.com/Jobs/Game-Designer

Video game designer jobs

https://www.ziprecruiter.com/Jobs/Game-Designer

Game developer jobs

https://www.ziprecruiter.com/Jobs/Game-Developer

Game tester jobs

https://www.ziprecruiter.com/Jobs/Game-Tester

Game tester jobs no experience

https://www.ziprecruiter.com/Jobs/Game-Tester-No-Experience

Game industry jobs

https://www.ziprecruiter.com/Jobs/Gaming-Industry

Graphic design internships

https://www.ziprecruiter.com/Jobs/Graphic-Design-Intern

Graphic designers near me

https://www.ziprecruiter.com/Jobs/Graphic-Designer

Graphic artist jobs

https://www.ziprecruiter.com/Jobs/Graphic-Designer

Information technology jobs near me

https://www.ziprecruiter.com/Jobs/Information-Technology

Instagram jobs

https://www.ziprecruiter.com/Jobs/Instagram

IT internships near me

https://www.ziprecruiter.com/Jobs/Internship

Computer science internships

https://www.ziprecruiter.com/Jobs/Internship-Computer-Science

IT audit jobs

https://www.ziprecruiter.com/Jobs/IT-Auditor

IT manager jobs

https://www.ziprecruiter.com/Jobs/IT-Director

IT director jobs

https://www.ziprecruiter.com/Jobs/IT-Director

Java developer jobs

https://www.ziprecruiter.com/Jobs/Java-Developer

System administrator jobs

https://www.ziprecruiter.com/Jobs/Junior-Systems-Administrator

Junior web developer jobs

https://www.ziprecruiter.com/Jobs/Junior-Web-Developer

Learning and development jobs

https://www.ziprecruiter.com/Jobs/Learning-and-Development-Manager

Mainframe jobs

https://www.ziprecruiter.com/Jobs/Mainframe

Market research analyst jobs

https://www.ziprecruiter.com/Jobs/Market-Research-Analyst

Research analyst jobs

https://www.ziprecruiter.com/Jobs/Market-Research-Analyst

Media jobs

https://www.ziprecruiter.com/Jobs/Media

Net developer

https://www.ziprecruiter.com/Jobs/NET-Developer

Network administrator jobs

https://www.ziprecruiter.com/Jobs/Network-Administrator

Network engineer jobs

https://www.ziprecruiter.com/Jobs/Network-Engineer

Networking jobs

https://www.ziprecruiter.com/Jobs/Network-Engineer

CCNA jobs with no experience

https://www.ziprecruiter.com/Jobs/No-Experience-CCNA

Computer jobs

https://www.ziprecruiter.com/Jobs/No-Experience-Computer

Entry level cyber security jobs no experience

https://www.ziprecruiter.com/Jobs/No-Experience-Cyber-Security

Online jobs hiring

https://www.ziprecruiter.com/Jobs/Online

Blogging jobs

https://www.ziprecruiter.com/Jobs/Online-Blogger

Online customer service jobs

https://www.ziprecruiter.com/Jobs/Online-Customer-Service-Representative

Online data entry jobs

https://www.ziprecruiter.com/Jobs/Online-Data-Entry

Online ESL jobs

https://www.ziprecruiter.com/Jobs/Online-ESL-Teacher

Freelance jobs online

https://www.ziprecruiter.com/Jobs/Online-Freelance

Freelance writing jobs online

https://www.ziprecruiter.com/Jobs/Online-Freelance-Writer

Online instructor jobs

https://www.ziprecruiter.com/Jobs/Online-Instructor

Online internships

https://www.ziprecruiter.com/Jobs/Online-Internship

Remote jobs online

https://www.ziprecruiter.com/Jobs/Online-Remote

Online customer service jobs

https://www.ziprecruiter.com/Jobs/Online-Support

Online tutoring jobs

https://www.ziprecruiter.com/Jobs/Online-Tutor

Online part time jobs from home

https://www.ziprecruiter.com/Jobs/Online-Work-From-Home

Oracle database administrator

https://www.ziprecruiter.com/Jobs/Oracle-Database-Administrator

Oracle DBA jobs

https://www.ziprecruiter.com/Jobs/Oracle-Database-Administrator

Part time data science jobs

https://www.ziprecruiter.com/Jobs/Part-Time-Data-Scientist

Part time virtual jobs

https://www.ziprecruiter.com/Jobs/Part-Time-Virtual

Peoplesoft jobs

https://www.ziprecruiter.com/Jobs/Peoplesoft

Podcast jobs

https://www.ziprecruiter.com/Jobs/Podcast

Podcast producer

https://www.ziprecruiter.com/Jobs/Podcast-Producer

Product development jobs

https://www.ziprecruiter.com/Jobs/Product-Development

Product engineer

https://www.ziprecruiter.com/Jobs/Product-Engineer

Always video gaming

https://www.ziprecruiter.com/Jobs/Professional-Video-Game-Tester

Python programming jobs

https://www.ziprecruiter.com/Jobs/Python-Programmer

QA analyst jobs

https://www.ziprecruiter.com/Jobs/QA-Analyst

Remote IT jobs

https://www.ziprecruiter.com/Jobs/Remote

Remote analyst jobs

https://www.ziprecruiter.com/Jobs/Remote-Analyst

AWS remote jobs

https://www.ziprecruiter.com/Jobs/Remote-AWS

Remote business analyst jobs

https://www.ziprecruiter.com/Jobs/Remote-Business-Analyst

Remote cad jobs

https://www.ziprecruiter.com/Jobs/Remote-CAD

Cobol programming jobs

https://www.ziprecruiter.com/Jobs/Remote-Cobol-Programmer

Remote copy editor jobs

https://www.ziprecruiter.com/Jobs/Remote-Copy-Editor

Remote cyber security jobs

https://www.ziprecruiter.com/Jobs/Remote-Cyber-Security

Cyber security consultant

https://www.ziprecruiter.com/Jobs/Remote-Cyber-Security-Consultant

Remote data analyst jobs

https://www.ziprecruiter.com/Jobs/Remote-Data-Analyst

Data engineer jobs

https://www.ziprecruiter.com/Jobs/Remote-Data-Engineer

Remote data entry

https://www.ziprecruiter.com/Jobs/Remote-Data-Entry

Remote data science jobs

https://www.ziprecruiter.com/Jobs/Remote-Data-Scientist

Remote developer jobs

https://www.ziprecruiter.com/Jobs/Remote-Developer

Remote web developer jobs

https://www.ziprecruiter.com/Jobs/Remote-Entry-Level-Web-Developer

Remote graphic design jobs

https://www.ziprecruiter.com/Jobs/Remote-Graphic-Designer

Health information technology jobs

https://www.ziprecruiter.com/Jobs/Remote-Health-Information-Technology

Help desk jobs

https://www.ziprecruiter.com/Jobs/Remote-Helpdesk

Remote internships

https://www.ziprecruiter.com/Jobs/Remote-Internship

Medical coding jobs

https://www.ziprecruiter.com/Jobs/Remote-Medical-Coder

Remote programming jobs

https://www.ziprecruiter.com/Jobs/Remote-Programmer

Salesforce admin jobs

https://www.ziprecruiter.com/Jobs/Remote-Salesforce-Administrator

Remote social media jobs

https://www.ziprecruiter.com/Jobs/Remote-Social-Media-Marketing-Manager

Remote software engineer jobs

https://www.ziprecruiter.com/Jobs/Remote-Software-Developer

Remote software engineer jobs

https://www.ziprecruiter.com/Jobs/Remote-Software-Engineer

Software sales jobs

https://www.ziprecruiter.com/Jobs/Remote-Software-Sales

IT support jobs

https://www.ziprecruiter.com/Jobs/Remote-Support

Remote technical writer

https://www.ziprecruiter.com/Jobs/Remote-Technical-Writer

Remote video editing jobs

https://www.ziprecruiter.com/Jobs/Remote-Video-Editor

Remote web developer jobs

https://www.ziprecruiter.com/Jobs/Remote-Web-Developer

Remote WordPress jobs

https://www.ziprecruiter.com/Jobs/Remote-wordpress-Developer

Work remotely jobs

https://www.ziprecruiter.com/Jobs/Remote-Work-From-Home

Remote work from home jobs

https://www.ziprecruiter.com/Jobs/Remote-Work-From-Home

Research assistant jobs

https://www.ziprecruiter.com/Jobs/Research-Assistant

Research jobs

https://www.ziprecruiter.com/Jobs/Researcher

Salesforce administrator jobs

https://www.ziprecruiter.com/Jobs/Salesforce-Administrator

Salesforce developer jobs

https://www.ziprecruiter.com/Jobs/Salesforce-Developer

Scrum Master jobs

https://www.ziprecruiter.com/Jobs/Scrum-Master

Social media manager jobs

https://www.ziprecruiter.com/Jobs/Social-Media-Manager

Software developer jobs

https://www.ziprecruiter.com/Jobs/Software-Developer

Software development manager

https://www.ziprecruiter.com/Jobs/Software-Development-Manager

Software engineer jobs

https://www.ziprecruiter.com/Jobs/Software-Engineer

Software intern

https://www.ziprecruiter.com/Jobs/Software-Engineer-Intern

Software developer internship

https://www.ziprecruiter.com/Jobs/Software-Engineer-Intern

Technical support specialist

https://www.ziprecruiter.com/Jobs/Technical-Support-Specialist

Technical support jobs

https://www.ziprecruiter.com/Jobs/Technical-Support-Specialist

Technical writer jobs

https://www.ziprecruiter.com/Jobs/Technical-Writer

Telecommunications jobs

https://www.ziprecruiter.com/Jobs/Telecommunications

Telecommuting jobs

https://www.ziprecruiter.com/Jobs/Telecommute

Telework jobs

https://www.ziprecruiter.com/Jobs/Telecommute

Telecommuting jobs near me

https://www.ziprecruiter.com/Jobs/Telecommute

Training and development jobs

https://www.ziprecruiter.com/Jobs/Training-and-Development-Manager

Video editor jobs

https://www.ziprecruiter.com/Jobs/Video-Editor

Video game tester jobs

https://www.ziprecruiter.com/Jobs/Video-Game-Tester

Game tester

https://www.ziprecruiter.com/Jobs/Video-Game-Tester

Game tester jobs at home

https://www.ziprecruiter.com/Jobs/Video-Game-Tester-From-Home

Video game tester jobs at home

https://www.ziprecruiter.com/Jobs/Video-Game-Tester-From-Home

Videographer jobs

https://www.ziprecruiter.com/Jobs/Videographer

Virtual jobs

https://www.ziprecruiter.com/Jobs/Virtual

Virtual administrative consultant

https://www.ziprecruiter.com/Jobs/Virtual-Administrative

Virtual administrative assistant

https://www.ziprecruiter.com/Jobs/Virtual-Administrative

Part time virtual assistant jobs

https://www.ziprecruiter.com/Jobs/Virtual-Assistant

Virtual customer service jobs

https://www.ziprecruiter.com/Jobs/Virtual-Customer-Service-Agent

Virtual customer service jobs

https://www.ziprecruiter.com/Jobs/Virtual-Customer-Service-Representative

Virtual data entry jobs

https://www.ziprecruiter.com/Jobs/Virtual-Data-Entry

Virtual jobs online

https://www.ziprecruiter.com/Jobs/Virtual-Online

Virtual support

https://www.ziprecruiter.com/Jobs/Virtual-Support

Virtual teaching jobs

https://www.ziprecruiter.com/Jobs/Virtual-Teacher

Virtual jobs from home

https://www.ziprecruiter.com/Jobs/Virtual-Work-From-Home

Web developer jobs

https://www.ziprecruiter.com/Jobs/Web-Developer

Web developer internship

https://www.ziprecruiter.com/Jobs/Web-Developer-Internship

Work from home jobs

https://www.ziprecruiter.com/Jobs/Work-From-Home

Working from home

https://www.ziprecruiter.com/Jobs/Work-From-Home

Work from home customer service jobs

https://www.ziprecruiter.com/Jobs/Work-From-Home

Ad posting jobs

https://www.ziprecruiter.com/Jobs/Work-From-Home-Ad-Posting

Computer jobs from home

https://www.ziprecruiter.com/Jobs/Work-From-Home-Computer

Jobs working from home on computer

https://www.ziprecruiter.com/Jobs/Work-From-Home-Computer

Travel agent jobs from home

https://www.ziprecruiter.com/Jobs/Work-From-Home-Corporate-Travel-Agent

Email processing jobs

https://www.ziprecruiter.com/Jobs/Work-From-Home-Email-Processing

Link posting jobs

Matthew Bulat

https://www.ziprecruiter.com/Jobs/Work-From-Home-Link-Posting

Virtual assistant jobs work from home

https://www.ziprecruiter.com/Jobs/Work-From-Home-Virtual-Assistant

Laptopjobs org

https://www.ziprecruiter.com/Jobs/Work-From-Laptop

129

13 ZIP RECRUITER IT ROLES BY POPULARITY (USA)

This shows IT Roles by Internet traffic in descending order. Which IT Role phrases are the most popular?

Work from home jobs, data entry jobs, working from home, cyber security jobs, comcast jobs, data analyst jobs, online tutoring jobs, medical coding jobs, telecommuting jobs, online data entry jobs, business analyst jobs, software engineer jobs, virtual jobs, freelance graphic designer, graphic designers near me, computer science internships, game tester, web developer jobs, game tester jobs, graphic design internships, Instagram jobs, computer jobs, research assistant jobs, video editor jobs, copywriter jobs, drone pilot jobs, entry level cyber security jobs, epic careers, work remotely jobs, remote work from home jobs, research jobs, software developer jobs, technical writer jobs, telecommunications jobs, video game tester jobs, business systems analyst, cyber security internships, esports jobs, flexible jobs, freelance web developer, remote graphic design jobs, work from home customer service jobs, audio engineering jobs, entry level software engineer, media jobs, online customer service jobs, freelance jobs online, freelance writing jobs online, online customer service jobs, online part time jobs from home, remote IT jobs, help desk jobs, social media manager jobs, blockchain jobs, computer consultant, animation jobs, ecommerce jobs, entry level computer science jobs, entry level computer science jobs, field service technician, game design jobs, NET developer, network engineer jobs, online jobs hiring, blogging jobs, product engineer, Scrum Master jobs, videographer jobs, entry level financial analyst, entry level work from home jobs, telework jobs, system administrator jobs, networking jobs, remote jobs online, software intern, software developer internship, telework jobs, web developer internship, computer jobs from home, CompTIA a+ jobs, computer technician jobs, intelligence analyst jobs, freelance web designer, game developer jobs, it manager jobs, learning and development jobs, network administrator jobs, online ESL jobs, cyber security consultant, salesforce admin jobs, remote social media jobs, it support jobs, software development manager, training and development jobs, virtual customer service jobs, virtual customer service jobs, travel agent jobs from home, 3d modelling jobs, computer engineering internships, desktop support jobs, DevOps jobs, video game designer jobs, java developer jobs, online instructor jobs, podcast jobs, podcast producer, product development jobs, remote data analyst jobs, data engineer jobs, remote developer jobs, remote web developer jobs, health information technology jobs, remote internships, remote software engineer jobs, remote software engineer jobs, remote web developer jobs, technical support specialist, jobs working from home on computer, computer forensics jobs, Excel jobs, digital marketing internship, entry level data analyst jobs, MIS jobs, game industry jobs, information technology jobs near me, IT internships near me, market research analyst jobs, research analyst jobs, Oracle DBA jobs, part time virtual jobs, remote programming jobs, software sales jobs, Salesforce administrator jobs, part time virtual assistant jobs, virtual teaching jobs, virtual jobs from home, game tester jobs at home, CISO jobs, entry level business analyst jobs, computer coding jobs, Python developer jobs, Salesforce entry level jobs, virtual assistant jobs for beginners, freelance videographer, graphic artist jobs, IT audit jobs, IT director jobs, junior web developer jobs, online internships, Python programming jobs, QA analyst jobs, Cobol programming jobs, remote cyber security jobs, Salesforce developer jobs, technical support jobs, game tester jobs at home, virtual administrative assistant, ad posting jobs, email processing jobs, network security jobs, computer support specialist jobs, entry level coding jobs, entry level Python jobs, remote business analyst jobs, remote copy editor jobs, remote data science jobs, remote video editing jobs, virtual jobs online, freelance content writer, mainframe jobs, Oracle database administrator, Peoplesoft jobs, remote analyst jobs, remote data entry, remote technical writer, video game tester jobs at home, virtual data entry jobs, laptopjobs org, video game tester from home, always video gaming, AWS remote jobs, remote WordPress jobs, telecommuting jobs near me, game tester jobs no experience, work from home flexible hours, entry level help desk, entry level technical writer jobs, active directory administrator, link posting jobs, virtual assistant jobs work from home, freelance computer programmer, part time data science jobs, remote cad jobs, virtual administrative consultant, computer coding jobs from home, front end specialist, CCNA jobs with no experience, entry level cyber security jobs no experience, virtual support

14 TOP 350+ ROLES IN IT ON FREELANCER (GLOBAL)

Freelancer has many task and project-based roles available globally. The digital tool for this chapter is https://itjobsformula.com/freelancer/

IT Role Keyword   **URL**

2d animation freelance work

https://www.freelancer.com/jobs/twod-animation/

3d architectural visualization freelance jobs

https://www.freelancer.com/jobs/rendering/

3d modelling work at home

https://www.freelancer.com/jobs/threed-modelling/

3d rendering jobs for freelancers

https://www.freelancer.com/jobs/rendering/

3ds Max freelance work

https://www.freelancer.com/jobs/threeds-max/

Access database developer freelance

https://www.freelancer.com/jobs/microsoft-access/

Adobe After Effects freelance

https://www.freelancer.com/jobs/after-effects/

AdSense jobs online

https://www.freelancer.com/jobs/google-adsense/

AI freelance jobs

https://www.freelancer.com/jobs/artificial-intelligence/

Analytics projects freelance

https://www.freelancer.com/jobs/analytics/

Android app development freelance projects

https://www.freelancer.com/jobs/android/

Angular freelance jobs

https://www.freelancer.com/jobs/angular-js/

Animation work

https://www.freelancer.com/jobs/animation/

App development freelance jobs

https://www.freelancer.com/jobs/app-developer/

App testing jobs online

https://www.freelancer.com/jobs/mobile-app-testing/

Arduino jobs

https://www.freelancer.com/jobs/arduino/

Article rewriting jobs online

https://www.freelancer.com/jobs/article-rewriting/

Artificial intelligence freelance

https://www.freelancer.com/jobs/artificial-intelligence/

ASP NET freelance jobs

https://www.freelancer.com/jobs/asp-net/

ASP NET MVC freelance jobs

https://www.freelancer.com/jobs/mvc/

AutoCAD freelance online

https://www.freelancer.com/jobs/autocad/

Autodesk Inventor freelance projects

https://www.freelancer.com/jobs/autodesk-inventor/

Automation freelance

https://www.freelancer.com/jobs/test-automation/

Azure freelance jobs

https://www.freelancer.com/jobs/azure/

Become a freelancer Facebook

https://www.freelancer.com/jobs/facebook-marketing/

BI freelance jobs

https://www.freelancer.com/jobs/business-intelligence/

BI freelance projects

https://www.freelancer.com/jobs/business-intelligence/

Bitcoin freelance

https://www.freelancer.com/jobs/bitcoin/

Biztalk freelance projects

https://www.freelancer.com/jobs/microsoft-biztalk/

Blockchain freelance projects

https://www.freelancer.com/jobs/blockchain/

Bootstrap freelance jobs

https://www.freelancer.com/jobs/twitter-bootstrap/

BTC freelancer

https://www.freelancer.com/jobs/bitcoin/

C freelance work

https://www.freelancer.com/jobs/c-programming/

C# programming jobs

https://www.freelancer.com/jobs/c-sharp-programming/

Cad drawing freelance

https://www.freelancer.com/jobs/autocad/

Cakephp freelancer

https://www.freelancer.com/jobs/cakephp/

Catia freelance jobs

https://www.freelancer.com/jobs/catia/

CGI freelancer

https://www.freelancer.com/jobs/computer-generated-images/

CodeIgniter freelance jobs

https://www.freelancer.com/jobs/codeigniter/

Coding freelance work

https://www.freelancer.com/jobs/coding/

ColdFusion freelance work

https://www.freelancer.com/jobs/cold-fusion/

Companies looking for new logos

https://www.freelancer.com/jobs/logo-design/

Content writing freelance work

https://www.freelancer.com/jobs/content-writing/

CorelDRAW work at home

https://www.freelancer.com/jobs/corel-draw/

Corona SDK freelancer

https://www.freelancer.com/job-search/corona-sdk/

Crystal reports freelance

https://www.freelancer.com/jobs/crystal-reports/

Data analytics freelance jobs

https://www.freelancer.com/jobs/data-analytics/

Data mining freelance

https://www.freelancer.com/jobs/data-mining/

Data science projects freelance

https://www.freelancer.com/jobs/data-science/

DBA freelance work

https://www.freelancer.com/jobs/database-administration/

Deep learning freelance jobs

https://www.freelancer.com/jobs/machine-learning/

Designer photoshop job

https://www.freelancer.com/jobs/photoshop-design/

Développeur full stack freelance

https://www.freelancer.com/jobs/full-stack-development/

Digital marketing freelance projects

https://www.freelancer.com/jobs/digital-marketing/

Django freelance projects

https://www.freelancer.com/jobs/django/

Dot NET freelance jobs

https://www.freelancer.com/jobs/dot-net/

Dot NET freelancer

https://www.freelancer.com/jobs/asp-net/

Dreamweaver freelancer

https://www.freelancer.com/jobs/dreamweaver/

Drone freelance

https://www.freelancer.com/jobs/drone-photography/

Drupal freelancer

https://www.freelancer.com/jobs/drupal/

Dynamics 365 freelancer

https://www.freelancer.com/jobs/microsoft-dynamics/

Dynamics CRM freelance jobs

https://www.freelancer.com/jobs/crm/

Ecommerce freelance

https://www.freelancer.com/jobs/ecommerce/

Email marketing freelancer

https://www.freelancer.com/jobs/email-marketing/

Embedded freelance

https://www.freelancer.com/jobs/embedded-software/

ERP freelance jobs

https://www.freelancer.com/jobs/erp/

Excel jobs online

https://www.freelancer.com/jobs/excel/

Excel macro freelance

https://www.freelancer.com/jobs/excel-macros/

Excel projects online

https://www.freelancer.com/jobs/excel/

Excel VBA jobs

https://www.freelancer.com/jobs/excel-vba/

Facebook API freelancer

https://www.freelancer.com/jobs/facebook-api/

Flash animation freelance work

https://www.freelancer.com/jobs/flash-animation/

Freelance 3d architectural visualization artist

https://www.freelancer.com/jobs/rendering/

Freelance access programmer

https://www.freelancer.com/jobs/microsoft-access/

Freelance adobe premiere jobs

https://www.freelancer.com/jobs/adobe-premiere-pro/

Freelance advertising design

https://www.freelancer.com/jobs/advertisement-design/

Freelance AdWords jobs

https://www.freelancer.com/jobs/google-adwords/

Freelance Amazon Web Services jobs

https://www.freelancer.com/jobs/amazon-web-services/

Freelance Android developer

https://www.freelancer.com/jobs/android/

Freelance Angular

https://www.freelancer.com/jobs/angular-js/

Freelance app design

https://www.freelancer.com/jobs/app-designer/

Freelance audio

https://www.freelancer.com/jobs/audio-production/

Freelance automation projects

https://www.freelancer.com/jobs/test-automation/

Freelance banner design jobs

https://www.freelancer.com/jobs/banner-design/

Freelance BI jobs

https://www.freelancer.com/jobs/business-intelligence/

Freelance bloggers wanted

https://www.freelancer.com/jobs/blog/

Freelance business analyst

https://www.freelancer.com/jobs/business-analysis/

Freelance C++ programming jobs

https://www.freelancer.com/jobs/cplusplus-programming/

Freelance cloud computing

https://www.freelancer.com/jobs/cloud-computing/

Freelance Cobol programming jobs

https://www.freelancer.com/jobs/cobol/

Freelance coding jobs

https://www.freelancer.com/jobs/coding/

Freelance coding jobs

https://www.freelancer.com/jobs/programming/

Freelance coding projects

https://www.freelancer.com/jobs/coding/

Freelance coding projects

https://www.freelancer.com/jobs/programming/

Freelance computer programming jobs

https://www.freelancer.com/jobs/programming/

Freelance computer security work

https://www.freelancer.com/jobs/computer-security/

Freelance computer support

https://www.freelancer.com/jobs/computer-help/

Freelance content writing jobs

https://www.freelancer.com/jobs/content-writing/

Freelance content writing projects

https://www.freelancer.com/jobs/content-writing/

Freelance cyber security jobs

https://www.freelancer.com/jobs/computer-security/

Freelance data analysis jobs

https://www.freelancer.com/jobs/data-analytics/

Freelance data analytics projects

https://www.freelancer.com/jobs/data-analytics/

Freelance data entry

https://www.freelancer.com/jobs/data-entry/

Freelance data scraping

https://www.freelancer.com/jobs/web-scraping/

Freelance database design

https://www.freelancer.com/jobs/database-development/

Freelance database developer jobs

https://www.freelancer.com/jobs/database-development/

Freelance database work

https://www.freelancer.com/jobs/database-development/

Freelance DBA jobs

https://www.freelancer.com/jobs/database-administration/

Freelance DBA projects

https://www.freelancer.com/jobs/database-administration/

Freelance Delphi

https://www.freelancer.com/jobs/delphi/

Freelance dot NET programmer

https://www.freelancer.com/jobs/dot-net/

Freelance dynamics CRM consultant

https://www.freelancer.com/jobs/crm/

Freelance ecommerce jobs

https://www.freelancer.com/jobs/ecommerce/

Freelance email developer

https://www.freelancer.com/jobs/email-developer/

Freelance email marketing jobs

https://www.freelancer.com/jobs/email-marketing/

Freelance embedded projects

https://www.freelancer.com/jobs/embedded-software/

Freelance embedded software engineer

https://www.freelancer.com/jobs/embedded-software/

Freelance excel projects

https://www.freelancer.com/jobs/excel/

Freelance flash animation jobs

https://www.freelancer.com/jobs/flash-animation/

Freelance front-end developer

https://www.freelancer.com/jobs/frontend-development/

Freelance game designer

https://www.freelancer.com/jobs/game-design/

Freelance game jobs

https://www.freelancer.com/jobs/game-development/

Freelance GIS digitizer

https://www.freelancer.com/job-search/freelance-gis-digitizing-work/

Freelance graphic artist needed

https://www.freelancer.com/jobs/graphic-design/

Freelance home based data entry jobs

https://www.freelancer.com/jobs/data-entry/

Freelance HTML CSS jobs

https://www.freelancer.com/jobs/html/

Freelance HTML designer

https://www.freelancer.com/jobs/html/

Freelance industrial design work

https://www.freelancer.com/jobs/product-design/

Freelance internet researcher

https://www.freelancer.com/jobs/internet-research/

Freelance iOS developer

https://www.freelancer.com/jobs/ios-development/

Freelance IT projects

https://www.freelancer.com/job/

Freelance J2EE

https://www.freelancer.com/jobs/j-ee/

Freelance Java programming jobs

https://www.freelancer.com/jobs/java/

Freelance java projects in India

https://www.freelancer.com/job-search/java-online-project-work-india/

Freelance JavaScript work

https://www.freelancer.com/jobs/javascript/

Freelance jobs 3d Max

https://www.freelancer.com/jobs/threeds-max/

Freelance jobs for Selenium testing

https://www.freelancer.com/jobs/selenium-webdriver/

Freelance jobs HTML5

https://www.freelancer.com/jobs/html-five/

Freelance jobs Machine Learning

https://www.freelancer.com/jobs/machine-learning/

Freelance Linux

https://www.freelancer.com/jobs/linux/

Freelance Linux programmer

https://www.freelancer.com/jobs/linux/

Freelance Machine Learning engineer

https://www.freelancer.com/jobs/machine-learning/

Freelance Machine Learning project

https://www.freelancer.com/jobs/machine-learning/

Freelance market research

https://www.freelancer.com/jobs/market-research/

Freelance mobile app testing

https://www.freelancer.com/jobs/mobile-app-testing/

Freelance NET developer

https://www.freelancer.com/jobs/dot-net/

Freelance Objective C

https://www.freelancer.com/jobs/objective-c/

Freelance Oracle consultant

https://www.freelancer.com/jobs/oracle/

Freelance Oracle developer

https://www.freelancer.com/jobs/oracle/

Freelance penetration testing jobs

https://www.freelancer.com/jobs/penetration-testing/

Freelance Peoplesoft

https://www.freelancer.com/jobs/peoplesoft/

Freelance photo editor

https://www.freelancer.com/jobs/photo-editing/

Freelance Photoshop jobs online

https://www.freelancer.com/jobs/photoshop/

Freelance PHP developer jobs

https://www.freelancer.com/jobs/php/

Freelance Pinterest

https://www.freelancer.com/jobs/pinterest/

Freelance ppt presentation

https://www.freelancer.com/jobs/powerpoint/

Freelance product designer

https://www.freelancer.com/jobs/product-design/

Freelance programming jobs

https://www.freelancer.com/jobs/programming/

Freelance programming projects

https://www.freelancer.com/jobs/programming/

Freelance project manager website

https://www.freelancer.com/jobs/project-management/

Freelance proof reader

https://www.freelancer.com/jobs/proofreading/

Freelance Python developer jobs

https://www.freelancer.com/jobs/python/

Freelance QA jobs

https://www.freelancer.com/jobs/testing-qa/

Freelance QA tester

https://www.freelancer.com/jobs/testing-qa/

Freelance QA testing projects

https://www.freelancer.com/jobs/testing-qa/

Freelance Raspberry Pi

https://www.freelancer.com/jobs/raspberry-pi/

Freelance React developer

https://www.freelancer.com/jobs/react-js/

Freelance report writing jobs

https://www.freelancer.com/jobs/report-writing/

Freelance robotics engineer

https://www.freelancer.com/jobs/robotics/

Freelance robotics jobs

https://www.freelancer.com/jobs/robotics/

Freelance Ruby on Rails developer

https://www.freelancer.com/jobs/ruby-on-rails/

Freelance ServiceNow jobs

https://www.freelancer.com/jobs/servicenow/

Freelance SharePoint consultants

https://www.freelancer.com/jobs/sharepoint/

Freelance SharePoint developer jobs

https://www.freelancer.com/jobs/sharepoint/

Freelance Siemens PLC programmer

https://www.freelancer.com/job-search/siemens-plc/

Freelance social media jobs

https://www.freelancer.com/jobs/social-media-marketing/

Freelance software development jobs

https://www.freelancer.com/jobs/software-development/

Freelance software jobs

https://www.freelancer.com/jobs/software-development/

Freelance software sales

https://www.freelancer.com/jobs/software-sales/

Freelance software tester

https://www.freelancer.com/jobs/software-testing/

Freelance software testing trainer

https://www.freelancer.com/jobs/software-testing/

Freelance Solidworks jobs online

https://www.freelancer.com/jobs/solidworks/

Freelance sound jobs

https://www.freelancer.com/jobs/audio-production/

Freelance SQL programmer

https://www.freelancer.com/jobs/sql/

Freelance SQL server

https://www.freelancer.com/jobs/sql/

Freelance SQL server developer

https://www.freelancer.com/jobs/microsoft-sql-server/

Freelance SSIS

https://www.freelancer.com/jobs/ssis/

Freelance Startup jobs

https://www.freelancer.com/jobs/startups/

Freelance statistical analysis

https://www.freelancer.com/jobs/statistical-analysis/

Freelance statistical analysis

https://www.freelancer.com/jobs/statistics/

Freelance Swift developer

https://www.freelancer.com/jobs/swift/

Freelance system administrator jobs

https://www.freelancer.com/jobs/system-admin/

Freelance system developer

https://www.freelancer.com/jobs/software-development/

Freelance Tableau

https://www.freelancer.com/jobs/tableau/

Freelance test automation projects

https://www.freelancer.com/jobs/test-automation/

Freelance testing websites

https://www.freelancer.com/jobs/website-testing/

Freelance tutoring websites

https://www.freelancer.com/jobs/education-tutoring/

Freelance usability testing

https://www.freelancer.com/jobs/usability-testing/

Freelance VBA developer

https://www.freelancer.com/jobs/excel-vba/

Freelance video editing services

https://www.freelancer.com/jobs/video-editing/

Freelance video game designer

https://www.freelancer.com/jobs/game-design/

Freelance video maker

https://www.freelancer.com/jobs/video-editing/

Freelance Videoscribe

https://www.freelancer.com/jobs/videoscribe/

Freelance virtual assistant

https://www.freelancer.com/jobs/virtual-assistant/

Freelance web app developer

https://www.freelancer.com/jobs/web-development/

Freelance web design work online

https://www.freelancer.com/jobs/website-design/

Freelance web dev jobs

https://www.freelancer.com/jobs/web-development/

Freelance web developer Germany

https://www.freelancer.com/freelancers/germany/html/

Freelance WordPress

https://www.freelancer.com/jobs/wordpress/

Freelance Zend

https://www.freelancer.com/jobs/zend/

Freelancer API

https://developers.freelancer.com/

Freelancer API

https://www.freelancer.com/jobs/api/

Freelancer AutoCAD 2d

https://www.freelancer.com/job-search/2d-autocad/

Freelancer content marketing

https://www.freelancer.com/jobs/content-marketing/

Freelancer customer care

https://www.freelancer.com/jobs/customer-support/

Freelancer dedicated server

https://www.freelancer.com/jobs/virtual-private-server/

Freelancer MIS jobs

https://www.freelancer.com/work/mis-reporting/

Freelancer MMO

https://www.freelancer.com/jobs/mmorpg/

Freelancer mobile app

https://www.freelancer.com/mobile

Freelancer mobile app developer

https://www.freelancer.com/jobs/app-developer/

Freelancer twitter

https://www.freelancer.com/jobs/twitter/

Freelancer UX design

https://www.freelancer.com/jobs/user-experience-design/

Freelancer Wikipedia

https://www.freelancer.com/jobs/wikipedia/

Freelancing jobs for front end developer

https://www.freelancer.com/jobs/frontend-development/

Freelancing websites for software testing

https://www.freelancer.com/jobs/software-testing/

Freelancing websites for software testing

https://www.freelancer.com/jobs/website-testing/

Game development freelance projects

https://www.freelancer.com/jobs/game-development/

Google ad jobs online

https://www.freelancer.com/jobs/google-adsense/

Google ads freelancer

https://www.freelancer.com/jobs/google-adwords/

Google AdSense jobs

https://www.freelancer.com/jobs/google-adsense/

Google AdWords freelancer

https://www.freelancer.com/jobs/google-adwords/

Google Analytics freelance jobs

https://www.freelancer.com/jobs/google-analytics/

Graphic design gigs

https://www.freelancer.com/jobs/graphic-design/

Growth hacker freelance

https://www.freelancer.com/jobs/growth-hacking/

Hire a website designer

https://www.freelancer.com/hire/website-design/

Hire Java developer

https://www.freelancer.com/hire/java/

Hire Java programmer online

https://www.freelancer.com/hire/java/

Hire JavaScript freelance

https://www.freelancer.com/hire/javascript/

Hire Linux developers

https://www.freelancer.com/hire/linux/

How to get a job in internet marketing

https://www.freelancer.com/jobs/internet-marketing/

How to get freelance animation work

https://www.freelancer.com/jobs/animation/

HTML freelance jobs

https://www.freelancer.com/jobs/html/

HTML5 freelance jobs

https://www.freelancer.com/jobs/html-five/

Indesign freelancer

https://www.freelancer.com/jobs/indesign/

Indesign work from home

https://www.freelancer.com/jobs/indesign/

Industrial automation freelance job

https://www.freelancer.com/jobs/plc-scada/

Informatica freelance jobs

https://www.freelancer.com/job-search/informatica/

Information security freelance

https://www.freelancer.com/jobs/computer-security/

Internet freelancer

https://www.freelancer.com/jobs/internet-marketing/

Inventor freelance jobs

https://www.freelancer.com/jobs/autodesk-inventor/

Ionic freelancer

https://www.freelancer.com/jobs/ionic-framework/

iOS freelance jobs

https://www.freelancer.com/jobs/ios-development/

iPad jobs

https://www.freelancer.com/jobs/ipad/

iPhone freelance projects

https://www.freelancer.com/jobs/ios-development/

Java freelance jobs online

https://www.freelancer.com/jobs/java/

JavaFX freelancer

https://www.freelancer.com/jobs/javafx/

JavaScript freelance projects

https://www.freelancer.com/jobs/javascript/

JavaScript online jobs

https://www.freelancer.com/jobs/javascript/

Jobs based on MS office

https://www.freelancer.com/jobs/microsoft-office/

Joomla freelance jobs

https://www.freelancer.com/jobs/joomla/

Joomla programmers for hire

https://www.freelancer.com/hire/joomla/

Junior Python developer freelance

https://www.freelancer.com/jobs/python/

Keyword research freelance jobs

https://www.freelancer.com/jobs/keyword-research/

LabVIEW freelance

https://www.freelancer.com/jobs/labview/

LabVIEW freelance projects

https://www.freelancer.com/jobs/labview/

Laravel freelance jobs

https://www.freelancer.com/jobs/laravel/

Latex freelance

https://www.freelancer.com/jobs/latex/

Liferay freelance jobs

https://www.freelancer.com/job-search/liferay/

Link building jobs online

https://www.freelancer.com/jobs/link-building/

Linux system administrator freelance jobs

https://www.freelancer.com/jobs/linux/

Logo design needed

https://www.freelancer.com/jobs/logo-design/

Looking for videographer

https://www.freelancer.com/jobs/videography/

Machine learning online jobs

https://www.freelancer.com/jobs/machine-learning/

Magento developer freelance

https://www.freelancer.com/jobs/magento/

Magento work

https://www.freelancer.com/jobs/magento/

Mailchimp freelancer

https://www.freelancer.com/jobs/mailchimp/

Managing Instagram accounts job

https://www.freelancer.com/jobs/instagram/

Market research projects online

https://www.freelancer.com/jobs/market-research/

MATLAB freelance work

https://www.freelancer.com/jobs/matlab-mathematica/

MATLAB programming jobs online

https://www.freelancer.com/jobs/matlab-mathematica/

Microsoft access programming jobs

https://www.freelancer.com/jobs/microsoft-access/

Microsoft excel consulting jobs

https://www.freelancer.com/jobs/excel/

Microsoft office jobs

https://www.freelancer.com/jobs/microsoft-office/

MicroStation freelancer

https://www.freelancer.com/jobs/microstation/

Midi programmer wanted

https://www.freelancer.com/job-search/midi-programmer/

MS office jobs online

https://www.freelancer.com/jobs/microsoft-office/

MS Word jobs

https://www.freelancer.com/jobs/word/

MySQL freelance jobs

https://www.freelancer.com/jobs/mysql/

Node JS developer freelance

https://www.freelancer.com/jobs/nodejs/

Node JS freelance projects

https://www.freelancer.com/jobs/nodejs/

Odoo freelance jobs

https://www.freelancer.com/jobs/odoo/

Online academic research writing jobs

https://www.freelancer.com/jobs/research-writing/

Online affiliate marketing jobs

https://www.freelancer.com/jobs/affiliate-marketing/

Online BPO

https://www.freelancer.com/jobs/bpo/

Online coding jobs in Java

https://www.freelancer.com/jobs/java/

Online documentation jobs

https://www.freelancer.com/jobs/documentation/

Online game design jobs

https://www.freelancer.com/jobs/game-design/

Online game development jobs

https://www.freelancer.com/jobs/game-development/

Online jobs for biotechnology students

https://www.freelancer.com/jobs/biotechnology/

Online jobs in digital marketing

https://www.freelancer.com/jobs/digital-marketing/

Online Machine Learning jobs

https://www.freelancer.com/jobs/machine-learning/

Online Photoshop jobs

https://www.freelancer.com/jobs/photoshop/

Online SEO projects jobs

https://www.freelancer.com/jobs/seo/

Online SEO work projects

https://www.freelancer.com/jobs/seo/

Online software projects for developers

https://www.freelancer.com/jobs/software-development/

Online video editing jobs

https://www.freelancer.com/jobs/video-editing/

Online web hosting jobs

https://www.freelancer.com/jobs/web-hosting/

OpenCart expert freelancer

https://www.freelancer.com/jobs/open-cart/

Oscommerce freelancer

https://www.freelancer.com/jobs/oscommerce/

Part time 3d renderer

https://www.freelancer.com/jobs/rendering/

PayPal freelancer

https://www.freelancer.com/jobs/paypal-api/

PhoneGap jobs

https://www.freelancer.com/jobs/phonegap/

Photoshop design work

https://www.freelancer.com/jobs/photoshop-design/

PHP freelancer needed

https://www.freelancer.com/jobs/php/

PHP online jobs

https://www.freelancer.com/jobs/php/

Pinterest freelance jobs

https://www.freelancer.com/jobs/pinterest/

Pl SQL freelance projects

https://www.freelancer.com/jobs/oracle/

PLC freelance

https://www.freelancer.com/jobs/plc-scada/

PLC programmer freelance work

https://www.freelancer.com/jobs/plc-scada/

PowerPoint jobs

https://www.freelancer.com/jobs/powerpoint/

PowerShell freelance

https://www.freelancer.com/jobs/powershell/

Prezi freelancer

https://www.freelancer.com/jobs/prezi/

Project writing jobs online

https://www.freelancer.com/jobs/online-writing/

Promoter jobs Instagram

https://www.freelancer.com/jobs/instagram/

Python developer freelance jobs

https://www.freelancer.com/jobs/python/

QlikView freelance projects

https://www.freelancer.com/jobs/qlikview/

R programming freelance jobs

https://www.freelancer.com/jobs/r-programming-language/

React developer freelance

https://www.freelancer.com/jobs/react-js/

Salesforce admin freelance jobs

https://www.freelancer.com/jobs/salesforce-com/

Salesforce freelance

https://www.freelancer.com/jobs/salesforce-com/

Salesforce projects online

https://www.freelancer.com/jobs/salesforce-com/

SAP ABAP freelance jobs

https://www.freelancer.com/jobs/sap/

SAP ABAP freelance projects

https://www.freelancer.com/jobs/sap/

SAP freelance jobs

https://www.freelancer.com/jobs/sap/

SAP freelancing projects

https://www.freelancer.com/jobs/sap/

SAS freelance jobs

https://www.freelancer.com/jobs/sas/

Scraping work

https://www.freelancer.com/jobs/web-scraping/

Search engine optimization freelance jobs

https://www.freelancer.com/jobs/seo/

Selenium freelance jobs

https://www.freelancer.com/jobs/selenium-webdriver/

SEO analyst freelance

https://www.freelancer.com/jobs/seo/

SEO freelancer

https://www.freelancer.com/jobs/seo/

SEO freelancer in India

https://www.freelancer.com/freelancers/india/seo/

SEO writing jobs

https://www.freelancer.com/jobs/seo-writing/

ServiceNow freelance work

https://www.freelancer.com/jobs/servicenow/

Shopify freelancer

https://www.freelancer.com/jobs/shopify-site/

Sketchup freelancer

https://www.freelancer.com/jobs/google-sketchup/

Social media marketing needed

https://www.freelancer.com/jobs/social-media-marketing/

Software development gigs

https://www.freelancer.com/jobs/software-development/

Software development projects freelance

https://www.freelancer.com/jobs/software-development/

Software development work

https://www.freelancer.com/jobs/software-development/

Software testing projects for freelancers

https://www.freelancer.com/jobs/software-testing/

Solidworks 3d modelling jobs

https://www.freelancer.com/jobs/solidworks/

Sound design work

https://www.freelancer.com/jobs/sound-design/

Spark freelancers

https://www.freelancer.com/jobs/spark/

Splunk freelance jobs

https://www.freelancer.com/jobs/splunk/

SSIS freelance jobs

https://www.freelancer.com/jobs/ssis/

Swift freelance jobs

https://www.freelancer.com/jobs/swift/

Symfony freelance jobs

https://www.freelancer.com/jobs/symfony-php/

Testing freelance projects

https://www.freelancer.com/jobs/software-testing/

Ui design freelance work

https://www.freelancer.com/jobs/ui-design/

Umbraco freelancer

https://www.freelancer.com/jobs/umbraco/

Unity 3d freelance

https://www.freelancer.com/jobs/unity-3d/

Unreal engine freelance jobs

https://www.freelancer.com/job-search/unreal-engine/

Unreal engine freelance jobs

https://www.freelancer.com/jobs/unreal-engine/

VBA work

https://www.freelancer.com/jobs/excel-vba/

Virtual worlds jobs

https://www.freelancer.com/jobs/virtual-worlds/

Visual basic 6.0 work online

https://www.freelancer.com/jobs/visual-basic/

Visual basic freelance work

https://www.freelancer.com/jobs/visual-basic/

Vuejs freelance

https://www.freelancer.com/jobs/vue-js/

Web application development freelance

https://www.freelancer.com/jobs/web-development/

Web design jobs online

https://www.freelancer.com/jobs/website-design/

Web design online work

https://www.freelancer.com/jobs/website-design/

Web design projects freelance

https://www.freelancer.com/jobs/website-design/

Web designer freelancer

https://www.freelancer.com/jobs/website-design/

Web research jobs

https://www.freelancer.com/jobs/internet-research/

Website creator job

https://www.freelancer.com/jobs/website-design/

WooCommerce freelancer

https://www.freelancer.com/jobs/woocommerce/

WordPress freelance jobs

https://www.freelancer.com/jobs/wordpress/

Www freelancer NET

https://www.freelancer.com/jobs/net/

Xml freelance jobs

https://www.freelancer.com/jobs/xml/

YouTube freelancer

https://www.freelancer.com/jobs/youtube/

YouTube jobs online

https://www.freelancer.com/jobs/youtube/

ZOHO freelancer

https://www.freelancer.com/jobs/zoho/

15 FREELANCER IT ROLES BY POPULARITY (GLOBAL)

This shows IT Roles by Internet traffic in descending order. Which IT activities are the most popular?

Freelance programming jobs, freelance data entry, SEO freelancer, freelance coding jobs, freelance coding jobs, freelance social media jobs, hire a website designer, freelance photo editor, logo design needed, online video editing jobs, freelance Android developer, freelance content writing jobs, freelance iOS developer, freelance product designer, Microsoft office jobs, freelance front end developer, freelance software tester, freelance virtual assistant, salesforce freelance, WordPress freelance jobs, Excel VBA jobs, freelance business analyst, freelance market research, freelance software jobs, PowerPoint jobs, YouTube jobs online, animation work, Arduino jobs, C# programming jobs, email marketing freelancer, Excel jobs online, freelance QA jobs, freelance WordPress, graphic design gigs, hire Java developer, online photoshop jobs, SEO writing jobs, Shopify freelancer, 3d architectural visualization freelance jobs, Angular freelance jobs, Azure freelance jobs, BI freelance projects, BTC freelancer, Corona SDK freelancer, ecommerce freelance, freelance AdWords jobs, freelance bloggers wanted, freelance data analytics projects, freelance Dot NET programmer, freelance HTML designer, freelance objective C, freelance Photoshop jobs online, freelance testing websites, freelancing websites for software testing, freelancing websites for software testing, game development freelance projects, market research projects online, MS word jobs, Oscommerce freelancer, PHP freelancer needed, PHP online jobs, pl SQL freelance projects, SAP ABAP freelance projects, SketchUp freelancer, Visual Basic 6.0 work online, web design jobs online, xml freelance jobs, AutoCAD freelance online, blockchain freelance projects, companies looking for new logos, data science projects freelance, Django freelance projects, embedded freelance, Excel projects online, freelance Adobe Premiere jobs, freelance IT projects, freelance QA tester, freelance ServiceNow jobs, freelance SharePoint developer jobs, freelance sound jobs, freelance SQL programmer, freelance SQL server, freelance system administrator jobs, freelance usability testing, freelancer content marketing, freelancer mobile app, freelancing jobs for front end developer, industrial automation freelance job, JavaScript freelance projects, LabVIEW freelance projects, Magento developer freelance, online academic research writing jobs, online affiliate marketing jobs, online game development jobs, OpenCart expert freelancer, PhoneGap jobs, virtual worlds jobs, web application development freelance, AdSense jobs online, become a freelancer Facebook, BI freelance jobs, bootstrap freelance jobs, C freelance work, cad drawing freelance, CorelDRAW work at home, digital marketing freelance projects, Dynamics 365 freelancer, Dynamics CRM freelance jobs, freelance Access programmer, freelance app design, freelance automation projects, freelance cloud computing, freelance coding projects, freelance coding projects, freelance email developer, freelance JavaScript work, freelance Linux programmer, freelance machine learning engineer, freelance test automation projects, freelance tutoring websites, freelance video maker, freelancer customer care, freelancer MIS jobs, google AdSense jobs, Joomla programmers for hire, junior Python developer freelance, looking for videographer, Midi programmer wanted, online web hosting jobs, PayPal freelancer, project writing jobs online, promoter jobs Instagram, Salesforce admin freelance jobs, SAP freelance jobs, scraping work, search engine optimization freelance jobs, Selenium freelance jobs, social media marketing needed, software development gigs, Splunk freelance jobs, Android app development freelance projects, app development freelance jobs, article rewriting jobs online, CGI freelancer, CodeIgniter freelance jobs, DBA freelance work, designer photoshop job, Flash animation freelance work, freelance 3d architectural visualization artist, freelance banner design jobs, freelance computer programming jobs, freelance data analysis jobs, freelance home based data entry jobs, freelance Java projects in India, freelance jobs 3d Max, freelance machine learning project, freelance NET developer, freelance Oracle consultant, freelance penetration testing jobs, freelance project manager website, freelance proof reader, freelance web design work online, freelancer dedicated server, Google AdWords freelancer, InDesign freelancer, InDesign work from home, iPad jobs, Java freelance jobs online, Javafx freelancer, Joomla freelance jobs, MATLAB programming jobs online, node JS freelance projects, Odoo freelance jobs, online documentation jobs, online game design jobs, online SEO work projects, part time 3d renderer, Photoshop design work, PLC freelance, PowerShell freelance, Prezi freelancer, SAS freelance jobs, Solidworks 3d modelling jobs, Spark freelancers, Swift freelance jobs, Unity 3d freelance, Unreal engine freelance jobs, Unreal engine freelance jobs, 2d animation freelance work, 3ds Max freelance work, Access database developer freelance, AI freelance jobs, analytics projects freelance, app testing jobs online, coding freelance work, content writing freelance work, data analytics freelance jobs, deep learning freelance jobs, développeur full stack freelance, ERP freelance jobs, freelance Amazon Web Services jobs, freelance audio, freelance C++ programming jobs, freelance computer security work, freelance cyber security jobs, freelance data scraping, freelance database design, freelance database developer jobs, freelance Delphi, freelance ecommerce jobs, freelance embedded software engineer, freelance GIS digitizer, freelance graphic artist needed, freelance industrial design work, freelance Java programming jobs, freelance jobs for Selenium testing, freelance jobs HTML5, freelance mobile app testing, freelance Python developer jobs, freelance robotics jobs, freelance Ruby on Rails developer, freelance software sales, freelance software testing trainer, freelance Solidworks jobs online, freelance SSIS, freelance system developer, freelance video editing services, freelance web dev jobs, freelance web developer Germany, freelancer AutoCAD 2d, freelancer mobile app developer, hire JavaScript freelance, information security freelance, inventor freelance jobs, iOS freelance jobs, keyword research freelance jobs, Liferay freelance jobs, Magento work, Mailchimp freelancer, MATLAB freelance work, Microsoft Access programming jobs, Node JS developer freelance, online BPO, online jobs for biotechnology students, online jobs in digital marketing, online machine learning jobs, Pinterest freelance jobs, PLC programmer freelance work, QlikView freelance projects, R programming freelance jobs, SAP ABAP freelance jobs, SEO analyst freelance, ServiceNow freelance work, software development work, sound design work, Symfony freelance jobs, 3d modelling work at home, 3d rendering jobs for freelancers, Adobe After Effects freelance, artificial intelligence freelance, ASP NET freelance jobs, ASP NET MVC freelance jobs, Autodesk Inventor freelance projects, automation freelance, Bitcoin freelance, Biztalk freelance projects, Cakephp freelancer, Catia freelance jobs, ColdFusion freelance work, Crystal Reports freelance, data mining freelance, Dot NET freelance jobs, Dot NET freelancer, Dreamweaver freelancer, drone freelance, Drupal freelancer, Excel macro freelance, Facebook API freelancer, freelance advertising design, freelance Angular, freelance BI jobs, freelance Cobol programming jobs, freelance computer support, freelance content writing projects, freelance database work, freelance DBA jobs, freelance DBA projects, freelance Dynamics CRM consultant, freelance email marketing jobs, freelance embedded projects, freelance Excel projects, freelance Flash animation jobs, freelance game designer, freelance game jobs, freelance HTML CSS jobs, freelance internet researcher, freelance J2ee, freelance jobs machine learning, freelance Linux, freelance Oracle developer, freelance PeopleSoft, freelance PHP developer jobs, freelance Pinterest, freelance ppt presentation, freelance programming projects, freelance QA testing projects, freelance Raspberry Pi, freelance React developer, freelance report writing jobs, freelance robotics engineer, freelance SharePoint consultants, freelance Siemens PLC programmer, freelance software development jobs, freelance SQL server developer, freelance Startup jobs, freelance statistical analysis, freelance statistical analysis, freelance Swift developer, freelance Tableau, freelance VBA developer, freelance video game designer, freelance Videoscribe, freelance web app developer, freelance Zend, freelancer API, freelancer API, freelancer MMO, freelancer Twitter, freelancer UX design, freelancer Wikipedia, Google ad jobs online, Google ads freelancer, Google Analytics freelance jobs, growth hacker freelance, hire Java programmer online, hire Linux developers, how to get a job in internet marketing, how to get freelance animation work, HTML freelance jobs, HTML5 freelance jobs, Informatica freelance jobs, Internet freelancer, Ionic freelancer, iPhone freelance projects, JavaScript online jobs, jobs based on MS Office, LabVIEW freelance, Laravel freelance jobs, Latex freelance, link building jobs online, Linux system administrator freelance jobs, machine learning online jobs, managing Instagram accounts job, Microsoft Excel consulting jobs, MicroStation freelancer, MS office jobs online, MySQL freelance jobs, online coding jobs in Java, online SEO projects jobs, online software projects for developers, Python developer freelance jobs, React developer freelance, Salesforce projects online, SAP freelancing projects, SEO freelancer in India, software development projects freelance, software testing projects for freelancers, SSIS freelance jobs, testing freelance projects, UI design freelance work, Umbraco freelancer, VBA work, Visual Basic freelance work, Vuejs freelance, web design online work, web design projects freelance, web designer freelancer, web research jobs, website creator job, WooCommerce freelancer, www freelancer net, YouTube freelancer, ZOHO freelancer

16 TOP 500+ ROLES IN IT ON UPWORK (GLOBAL)

Upwork has many short term and project IT Roles. Upwork is a new company from the merger of Odesk and Elance. The digital tool for this chapter is https://itjobsformula.com/upwork/

IT Role Keyword   **URL**

2d animation jobs freelance

https://www.upwork.com/o/jobs/browse/skill/2d-animation/

2d animation work from home

https://www.upwork.com/freelance-jobs/animation/

3d animation work

https://www.upwork.com/freelance-jobs/3d-animation/

3d architectural visualization freelance jobs

https://www.upwork.com/o/jobs/browse/?q=3d+architectural+visualization

3d conversion jobs

https://www.upwork.com/o/jobs/browse/?q=3d+conversion

3d design jobs online

https://www.upwork.com/freelance-jobs/3d-design/

3d design jobs online

https://www.upwork.com/o/jobs/browse/skill/3d-design/

3d freelance jobs online

https://www.upwork.com/freelance-jobs/3d-modeling/

3d outsourcing jobs

https://www.upwork.com/o/jobs/browse/?q=3d+outsourcing

3d rendering jobs for freelancers

https://www.upwork.com/o/jobs/browse/skill/3d-rendering/

3d visualizer freelance jobs

https://www.upwork.com/freelance-jobs/3d-visualizations/

3ds max designer jobs

https://www.upwork.com/freelance-jobs/3ds-max/

3ds max modelling jobs

https://www.upwork.com/o/jobs/browse/skill/3ds-max/

ABAP freelance opportunities

https://www.upwork.com/freelance-jobs/sap-abap/

Admin online

https://www.upwork.com/o/jobs/browse/c/admin-support/

Adobe InDesign jobs

https://www.upwork.com/freelance-jobs/adobe-indesign/

Adobe Photoshop freelance work

https://www.upwork.com/freelance-jobs/adobe-photoshop/

AdSense jobs online

https://www.upwork.com/freelance-jobs/google-adsense/

After Effects freelance work

https://www.upwork.com/freelance-jobs/adobe-after-effects/

AI freelance jobs

https://www.upwork.com/freelance-jobs/artificial-intelligence/

Android app development online jobs

https://www.upwork.com/freelance-jobs/android-app-development/

Android app development online jobs

https://www.upwork.com/o/jobs/browse/skill/android-app-development/

Angular 2 freelance jobs

https://www.upwork.com/o/jobs/browse/skill/angular2/

Angular freelance jobs

https://www.upwork.com/freelance-jobs/angular/

Angular freelance jobs

https://www.upwork.com/freelance-jobs/angularjs/

Animation work

https://www.upwork.com/freelance-jobs/animation/

Ansys freelance

https://www.upwork.com/freelance-jobs/ansys/

App promotion jobs

https://www.upwork.com/o/jobs/browse/?q=app+promotions

App testing jobs online

https://www.upwork.com/freelance-jobs/mobile-app-testing/

ArcGIS freelance jobs

https://www.upwork.com/o/jobs/browse/?q=arcgis+mapping

ArcGIS freelance jobs

https://www.upwork.com/o/jobs/browse/skill/arcgis/

ArcGIS online jobs

https://www.upwork.com/freelance-jobs/arcgis/

Arduino freelance jobs

https://www.upwork.com/freelance-jobs/arduino/

Asp NET freelance work

https://www.upwork.com/freelance-jobs/aspnet/

Asp NET MVC freelance jobs

https://www.upwork.com/freelance-jobs/aspnet-mvc/

Asp NET MVC freelance jobs

https://www.upwork.com/o/jobs/browse/skill/mvc/

Autodesk Fusion jobs

https://www.upwork.com/o/jobs/browse/skill/fusion-360/

Autodesk Inventor freelance projects

https://www.upwork.com/o/jobs/browse/skill/autodesk-inventor/

Autodesk Inventor work from home

https://www.upwork.com/freelance-jobs/autodesk-inventor/

Automation freelance

https://www.upwork.com/freelance-jobs/automated-testing/

Automation freelance

https://www.upwork.com/freelance-jobs/automation/

AWS freelance work

https://www.upwork.com/o/jobs/browse/skill/amazon-web-services/

Azure freelance jobs

https://www.upwork.com/freelance-jobs/azure/

Backend freelance

https://www.upwork.com/freelance-jobs/backend-rest-api/

Bash scripting jobs

https://www.upwork.com/freelance-jobs/bash-shell-scripting/

BI freelance jobs

https://www.upwork.com/freelance-jobs/business-intelligence/

Bitcoin freelance

https://www.upwork.com/freelance-jobs/bitcoin/

Blender 3d freelance

https://www.upwork.com/o/jobs/browse/skill/blender3d/

Blender 3d freelance jobs

https://www.upwork.com/freelance-jobs/blender3d/

Blockchain developer freelance

https://www.upwork.com/o/jobs/browse/skill/blockchain/

Blockchain freelance projects

https://www.upwork.com/freelance-jobs/blockchain/

Build website freelance

https://www.upwork.com/o/jobs/browse/?q=build+website

Business development consultant freelance

https://www.upwork.com/freelance-jobs/business-development/

Business objects freelance jobs

https://www.upwork.com/o/jobs/browse/?q=sap+business+objects

C# online jobs

https://www.upwork.com/freelance-jobs/c-sharp/

CAD design from home

https://www.upwork.com/o/jobs/browse/skill/cad-design/

CAE freelance jobs

https://www.upwork.com/freelance-jobs/cae-software/

Catia freelance jobs

https://www.upwork.com/o/jobs/browse/skill/catia/

Clickfunnels freelancer

https://www.upwork.com/o/jobs/browse/skill/clickfunnels/

Clojure freelance jobs

https://www.upwork.com/o/jobs/browse/skill/clojure/

CNC programming from home

https://www.upwork.com/freelance-jobs/cnc-programming/

ColdFusion freelance projects

https://www.upwork.com/freelance-jobs/coldfusion/

ColdFusion freelance work

https://www.upwork.com/o/jobs/browse/skill/coldfusion/

Companies looking for video production

https://www.upwork.com/freelance-jobs/video-production/

Computer repair work

https://www.upwork.com/o/jobs/browse/skill/computer-repair/

Computer technician for hire

https://www.upwork.com/hire/computer-technicians/

Computer vision freelance jobs

https://www.upwork.com/o/jobs/browse/skill/computer-vision/

Content writing freelance work

https://www.upwork.com/freelance-jobs/content-writing/

Copywriting work

https://www.upwork.com/freelance-jobs/copywriting/

Core Java freelance jobs

https://www.upwork.com/o/jobs/browse/skill/core-java/

Core PHP jobs

https://www.upwork.com/freelance-jobs/core-php/

Corel draw jobs online

https://www.upwork.com/freelance-jobs/corel-draw/

Creo freelance jobs

https://www.upwork.com/o/jobs/browse/skill/creo/

D3 JS freelance

https://www.upwork.com/freelance-jobs/d3-js/

Data collection freelancer

https://www.upwork.com/freelance-jobs/data-collection/

Data encoder online

https://www.upwork.com/o/jobs/browse/skill/data-encoding/

Data mining freelance

https://www.upwork.com/freelance-jobs/data-mining/

Data science freelance

https://www.upwork.com/freelance-jobs/data-science/

Data visualization freelance

https://www.upwork.com/freelance-jobs/data-visualization/

DBA freelance work

https://www.upwork.com/freelance-jobs/database-administration/

Deep Learning freelance jobs

https://www.upwork.com/o/jobs/browse/skill/deep-learning/

Delphi freelance work

https://www.upwork.com/freelance-jobs/delphi/

DevOps freelance jobs

https://www.upwork.com/o/jobs/browse/skill/devops/

Digital marketing freelance projects

https://www.upwork.com/freelance-jobs/internet-marketing/

Digital marketing Upwork profile

https://www.upwork.com/freelance-jobs/digital-marketing/

Django freelance projects

https://www.upwork.com/freelance-jobs/django/

Dot NET freelance jobs

https://www.upwork.com/o/jobs/browse/?q=dotnet

Dot NET freelancer

https://www.upwork.com/freelance-jobs/aspnet/

DTP jobs work from home

https://www.upwork.com/o/jobs/browse/?q=dtp

Dynamics AX freelance jobs

https://www.upwork.com/o/jobs/browse/skill/microsoft-dynamics/

Dynamics CRM freelance jobs

https://www.upwork.com/freelance-jobs/microsoft-dynamics-crm/

Dynamics nav freelance jobs

https://www.upwork.com/o/jobs/browse/?q=dynamics+nav

Editor needed for YouTube

https://www.upwork.com/o/jobs/browse/?q=editor+video+youtube

Email marketing Upwork

https://www.upwork.com/o/jobs/browse/skill/email-marketing/

ERP freelance jobs

https://www.upwork.com/o/jobs/browse/skill/erp/

ERP freelancer

https://www.upwork.com/freelance-jobs/erp/

Ethereum freelance jobs

https://www.upwork.com/freelance-jobs/ethereum/

ETL freelance jobs

https://www.upwork.com/o/jobs/browse/skill/data-extraction/

ETL freelance jobs

https://www.upwork.com/o/jobs/browse/skill/etl/

Excel freelance jobs

https://www.upwork.com/freelance-jobs/microsoft-excel/

Excel spreadsheet freelance work

https://www.upwork.com/freelance-jobs/spreadsheets/

Facebook ads manager freelance

https://www.upwork.com/freelance-jobs/facebook-ads/

Facebook API freelancer

https://www.upwork.com/o/jobs/browse/skill/facebook-api/

Flash animation freelance work

https://www.upwork.com/o/jobs/browse/?q=flash+animation

Forum posting jobs

https://www.upwork.com/freelance-jobs/forum-posting/

Freelance 2d animation jobs

https://www.upwork.com/freelance-jobs/2d-animation/

Freelance 3d modelling

https://www.upwork.com/o/jobs/browse/skill/3d-modeling/

Freelance 3d printing jobs

https://www.upwork.com/freelance-jobs/3d-printing/

Freelance 3d projects

https://www.upwork.com/freelance-jobs/3d-modeling/

Freelance academic writing jobs online

https://www.upwork.com/o/jobs/browse/skill/academic-writing

Freelance admin jobs online

https://www.upwork.com/freelance-jobs/administrative-support/

Freelance AdWords

https://www.upwork.com/freelance-jobs/goolge-adwords/

Freelance Android application developer

https://www.upwork.com/o/jobs/browse/skill/android-app-development/

Freelance Angular

https://www.upwork.com/freelance-jobs/angular-6/

Freelance Angular 2 developer

https://www.upwork.com/o/jobs/browse/skill/angular2/

Freelance animation projects

https://www.upwork.com/o/jobs/browse/skill/animation/

Freelance audio editing jobs

https://www.upwork.com/o/jobs/browse/skill/sound-editing/

Freelance audio jobs

https://www.upwork.com/freelance-jobs/audio-production/

Freelance AutoCAD jobs

https://www.upwork.com/freelance-jobs/autocad/

Freelance AutoCAD jobs from home

https://www.upwork.com/o/jobs/browse/skill/autocad/

Freelance automation projects

https://www.upwork.com/freelance-jobs/test-automation/

Freelance automation testing jobs

https://www.upwork.com/freelance-jobs/automated-testing/

Freelance big data engineer

https://www.upwork.com/o/jobs/browse/skill/big-data/

Freelance blog writer

https://www.upwork.com/o/jobs/browse/skill/blog-writing/

Freelance business analyst

https://www.upwork.com/freelance-jobs/business-analysis/

Freelance business development jobs

https://www.upwork.com/freelance-jobs/business-development/

Freelance C++ programming jobs

https://www.upwork.com/freelance-jobs/c-plus-plus/

Freelance CAD designer jobs

https://www.upwork.com/o/jobs/browse/skill/cad-design/

Freelance CAD work

https://www.upwork.com/freelance-jobs/cad-design/

Freelance Catia

https://www.upwork.com/freelance-jobs/catia/

Freelance cloud consultant

https://www.upwork.com/freelance-jobs/cloud-computing/

Freelance CNC programming

https://www.upwork.com/hire/cnc-programmers/

Freelance CNC work

https://www.upwork.com/o/jobs/browse/skill/cnc-programming/

Freelance code work

https://www.upwork.com/freelance-jobs/infrastructure-as-code/

Freelance communications jobs

https://www.upwork.com/freelance-jobs/communications/

Freelance computer engineer

https://www.upwork.com/o/jobs/browse/skill/computer-engineering/

Freelance computer jobs from home

https://www.upwork.com/o/jobs/browse/skill/computer-skills/

Freelance content creator

https://www.upwork.com/freelance-jobs/content-creation/

Freelance content developer

https://www.upwork.com/freelance-jobs/content-development/

Freelance copywriter website

https://www.upwork.com/o/jobs/browse/?q=copywriting+website

Freelance CSS designer

https://www.upwork.com/freelance-jobs/css/

Freelance cyber security jobs

https://www.upwork.com/freelance-jobs/security-engineering/

Freelance data analysis

https://www.upwork.com/o/jobs/browse/skill/data-analysis/

Freelance data analytics projects

https://www.upwork.com/freelance-jobs/data-analysis/

Freelance data capturing

https://www.upwork.com/o/jobs/browse/?q=capture+data

Freelance data collection jobs

https://www.upwork.com/o/jobs/browse/skill/data-collection/

Freelance data jobs

https://www.upwork.com/freelance-jobs/data-entry/

Freelance data scientist

https://www.upwork.com/o/jobs/browse/skill/data-science/

Freelance database design

https://www.upwork.com/o/jobs/browse/skill/database-design/

Freelance database developer jobs

https://www.upwork.com/o/jobs/browse/skill/database-programming/

Freelance database jobs

https://www.upwork.com/freelance-jobs/database-design/

Freelance development consultant

https://www.upwork.com/o/jobs/browse/?q=consultant+software

Freelance digital marketing services

https://www.upwork.com/o/jobs/browse/?q=digital+marketing+service
s

Freelance documentation

https://www.upwork.com/freelance-jobs/technical-documentation/

Freelance ecommerce jobs

https://www.upwork.com/freelance-jobs/ecommerce-consulting/

Freelance ecommerce manager

https://www.upwork.com/o/jobs/browse/?q=ecommerce+managemen
t+project

Freelance eLearning jobs

https://www.upwork.com/freelance-jobs/e-learning/

Freelance email copywriter

https://www.upwork.com/o/jobs/browse/skill/email-copywriting/

Freelance email designer

https://www.upwork.com/freelance-jobs/email-design/

Freelance embedded programmer

https://www.upwork.com/o/jobs/browse/?q=embedded+programming
+systems

Freelance embedded projects

https://www.upwork.com/o/jobs/browse/skill/embedded-systems/

Freelance embedded software developer

https://www.upwork.com/freelance-jobs/embedded-c/

Freelance embedded software engineer

https://www.upwork.com/o/jobs/browse/skill/embedded-c/

Freelance Excel consultant

https://www.upwork.com/freelance-jobs/microsoft-excel/

Freelance Facebook marketing

https://www.upwork.com/freelance-jobs/facebook-marketing/

Freelance Flash animation jobs

https://www.upwork.com/o/jobs/browse/skill/flash-animation/

Freelance front end developer work

https://www.upwork.com/freelance-jobs/frontend-development/

Freelance front end web developer jobs

https://www.upwork.com/freelance-jobs/frontend-development/

Freelance Fusion 360 jobs

https://www.upwork.com/o/jobs/browse/?q=fusion+360

Freelance game designer

https://www.upwork.com/freelance-jobs/game-design/

Freelance GIS jobs online

https://www.upwork.com/freelance-jobs/gis/

Freelance GIS specialist

https://www.upwork.com/o/jobs/browse/?q=gis+mapping

Freelance graphic design work

https://www.upwork.com/freelance-jobs/graphic-design/

Freelance graphic jobs online

https://www.upwork.com/o/jobs/browse/c/design-creative/sc/graphics-design/

Freelance Hadoop developer

https://www.upwork.com/o/jobs/browse/skill/hadoop/

Freelance help desk jobs

https://www.upwork.com/freelance-jobs/helpdesk-support/

Freelance help desk support

https://www.upwork.com/o/jobs/browse/skill/helpdesk-support/

Freelance HTML coding jobs

https://www.upwork.com/freelance-jobs/html/

Freelance HTML5 game developer
https://www.upwork.com/o/jobs/browse/?q=html5%2c+game+develop
ment%2c+game+programming

Freelance Internet researcher

https://www.upwork.com/freelance-jobs/internet-research/

Freelance iOS developer

https://www.upwork.com/o/jobs/browse/skill/ios-development/

Freelance iPhone app developer

https://www.upwork.com/hire/iphone-app-developers/

Freelance IT jobs

https://www.upwork.com/o/jobs/browse/c/it-networking/

Freelance IT projects

https://www.upwork.com/freelance-jobs/project-management/

Freelance IT solutions

https://www.upwork.com/o/jobs/browse/?q=it+solutions

Freelance IT support jobs

https://www.upwork.com/freelance-jobs/technical-support/

Freelance Java J2ee projects

https://www.upwork.com/o/jobs/browse/skill/j2ee/

Freelance Java programming work

https://www.upwork.com/freelance-jobs/java/

Freelance JavaScript jobs

https://www.upwork.com/freelance-jobs/javascript/

Freelance jobs for Selenium testing

https://www.upwork.com/o/jobs/browse/?q=selenium+testing

Freelance jobs machine learning

https://www.upwork.com/o/jobs/browse/c/data-science-analytics/sc/machine-learning/

Freelance jobs PowerPoint presentation

https://www.upwork.com/freelance-jobs/microsoft-powerpoint/

Freelance Joomla jobs

https://www.upwork.com/o/jobs/browse/skill/joomla/

Freelance Linux

https://www.upwork.com/freelance-jobs/linux/

Freelance machine learning project

https://www.upwork.com/o/jobs/browse/skill/machine-learning/

Freelance marketing research jobs

https://www.upwork.com/freelance-jobs/market-research/

Freelance media production

https://www.upwork.com/o/jobs/browse/?q=media+production

Freelance mobile app testing

https://www.upwork.com/freelance-jobs/mobile-app-testing/

Freelance MS Access jobs

https://www.upwork.com/o/jobs/browse/skill/microsoft-access/

Freelance MS Project

https://www.upwork.com/o/jobs/browse/skill/microsoft-project/

Freelance network technician

https://www.upwork.com/o/jobs/browse/?q=computer+network+technician

Freelance newsletter writer

https://www.upwork.com/o/jobs/browse/skill/newsletter-writing/

Freelance objective C

https://www.upwork.com/freelance-jobs/objective-c/

Freelance operations consultant

https://www.upwork.com/freelance-jobs/operations-management/

Freelance penetration testing jobs

https://www.upwork.com/freelance-jobs/penetration-testing/

Freelance photo editing online

https://www.upwork.com/o/jobs/browse/skill/photo-editing/

Freelance PHP MySQL programmer

https://www.upwork.com/o/jobs/browse/?q=php.+mysql

Freelance PHP MySQL programmer

https://www.upwork.com/o/jobs/browse/?q=php+programmer

Freelance PL SQL developer

https://www.upwork.com/freelance-jobs/oracle-plsql/

Freelance PMP

https://www.upwork.com/o/jobs/browse/skill/project-management/

Freelance podcast editor jobs

https://www.upwork.com/o/jobs/browse/?q=editing+podcast

Freelance process engineer

https://www.upwork.com/o/jobs/browse/skill/process-engineering/

Freelance product developer

https://www.upwork.com/o/jobs/browse/skill/product-development/

Freelance product development

https://www.upwork.com/freelance-jobs/product-development/

Freelance product manager jobs

https://www.upwork.com/o/jobs/browse/skill/product-management/

Freelance Python developer jobs

https://www.upwork.com/freelance-jobs/python/

Freelance QA testing projects

https://www.upwork.com/o/jobs/browse/c/web-mobile-software-dev/sc/qa-testing/

Freelance R programming

https://www.upwork.com/freelance-jobs/r/

Freelance React developer

https://www.upwork.com/freelance-jobs/react-js/

Freelance rendering jobs

https://www.upwork.com/freelance-jobs/3d-rendering/

Freelance report writing jobs

https://www.upwork.com/o/jobs/browse/skill/report-writing/

Freelance reporting services

https://www.upwork.com/o/jobs/browse/?q=reporting+services

Freelance research projects

https://www.upwork.com/o/jobs/browse/skill/research/

Freelance RPA

https://www.upwork.com/o/jobs/browse/skill/robotic-process-automation/

Freelance Ruby programmer

https://www.upwork.com/freelance-jobs/ruby-on-rails/

Freelance SEO content writing jobs

https://www.upwork.com/freelance-jobs/seo-writing/

Freelance SEO jobs

https://www.upwork.com/freelance-jobs/seo/

Freelance SharePoint consultants

https://www.upwork.com/o/jobs/browse/skill/microsoft-sharepoint-development/

Freelance SharePoint developer jobs

https://www.upwork.com/freelance-jobs/sharepoint/

Freelance Six Sigma jobs

https://www.upwork.com/o/jobs/browse/?q=lean+sigma

Freelance social media content creator

https://www.upwork.com/freelance-jobs/content-creation/

Freelance social media designer

https://www.upwork.com/o/jobs/browse/skill/social-media-design/

Freelance social media jobs

https://www.upwork.com/o/jobs/browse/skill/social-media-marketing/

Freelance social media marketing manager

https://www.upwork.com/freelance-jobs/social-media-marketing/

Freelance SQL server developer

https://www.upwork.com/o/jobs/browse/skill/microsoft-sql-server-development/

Freelance Startup jobs

https://www.upwork.com/freelance-jobs/startup/

Freelance statistical analysis

https://www.upwork.com/o/jobs/browse/skill/statistical-analysis/

Freelance statistical analysis

https://www.upwork.com/o/jobs/browse/skill/statistics/

Freelance sysadmin jobs

https://www.upwork.com/o/jobs/browse/?q=sysadmin

Freelance system administrator jobs

https://www.upwork.com/freelance-jobs/system-administration/

Freelance system developer

https://www.upwork.com/o/jobs/browse/?q=developer+system

Freelance Tableau consulting

https://www.upwork.com/freelance-jobs/tableau/

Freelance tech work

https://www.upwork.com/o/jobs/browse/?q=tech

Freelance technical support jobs

https://www.upwork.com/o/jobs/browse/c/customer-service/sc/technical-support/

Freelance technical writer wanted

https://www.upwork.com/o/jobs/browse/skill/technical-writing/

Freelance telecom jobs

https://www.upwork.com/o/jobs/browse/skill/telecommunications-engineering/

Freelance Unity programmer

https://www.upwork.com/freelance-jobs/unity-3d/

Freelance usability

https://www.upwork.com/o/jobs/browse/skill/usability-testing

Freelance video editing jobs

https://www.upwork.com/o/jobs/browse/skill/video-editing/

Freelance video game designer

https://www.upwork.com/o/jobs/browse/skill/game-design/

Freelance videographer

https://www.upwork.com/o/jobs/browse/skill/videography/

Freelance virtual assistant jobs

https://www.upwork.com/o/jobs/browse/skill/virtual-assistant/

Freelance web application projects

https://www.upwork.com/o/jobs/browse/?q=application+project+web

Freelance web content

https://www.upwork.com/o/jobs/browse/skill/web-content-management/

Freelance web design jobs

https://www.upwork.com/o/jobs/browse/skill/web-design/

Freelance web design jobs for beginners

https://www.upwork.com/freelance-jobs/web-design/

Freelance web developer

https://www.upwork.com/freelance-jobs/frontend-development/

Freelance web developer jobs

https://www.upwork.com/o/jobs/browse/c/web-mobile-software-dev/sc/web-development/

Freelance web developer wanted

https://www.upwork.com/freelance-jobs/frontend-development/

Freelance webmaster

https://www.upwork.com/o/jobs/browse/?q=webmaster

Freelancer chatbot

https://www.upwork.com/freelance-jobs/chatbot-development/

Freelancer content marketing

https://www.upwork.com/freelance-jobs/content-marketing/

Freelancer MIS jobs

https://www.upwork.com/o/jobs/browse/?q=mis

Fusion 360 freelance

https://www.upwork.com/freelance-jobs/fusion-360/

Game developer needed

https://www.upwork.com/freelance-jobs/game-development/

Game developer Upwork

https://www.upwork.com/o/jobs/browse/c/web-mobile-software-dev/sc/game-development/

Game development freelance projects

https://www.upwork.com/freelance-jobs/game-programming/

Game streaming jobs

https://www.upwork.com/o/jobs/browse/skill/video-streaming/

GIS freelance

https://www.upwork.com/freelance-jobs/gis/

Golang freelance jobs

https://www.upwork.com/freelance-jobs/golang/

Google ad jobs online

https://www.upwork.com/o/jobs/browse/skill/google-adsense/

Google AdWords work from home

https://www.upwork.com/freelance-jobs/google-adwords/

Google analytics Upwork

https://www.upwork.com/freelance-jobs/google-analytics/

Graphic design work

https://www.upwork.com/o/jobs/browse/c/design-creative/sc/graphics-design/

Graphic designer needed for logo

https://www.upwork.com/freelance-jobs/logo-design/

Graphic work online

https://www.upwork.com/o/jobs/browse/skill/graphic-design/

Hadoop freelance jobs

https://www.upwork.com/freelance-jobs/hadoop/

Hadoop freelance jobs

https://www.upwork.com/o/jobs/browse/skill/hadoop/

Hardware freelancer

https://www.upwork.com/freelance-jobs/hardware-troubleshooting/

Hire Etsy expert

https://www.upwork.com/hire/etsy-administration-freelancers/

Hire Facebook marketing expert

https://www.upwork.com/hire/facebook-ads-freelancers/

Hire iOS developer

https://www.upwork.com/hire/ios-developers/

Hire Java programmer online

https://www.upwork.com/hire/java-developers/

Hire PhoneGap developer

https://www.upwork.com/hire/phonegap-developers/

Hire Wix developer

https://www.upwork.com/hire/wix-freelancers/

Home based content moderator

https://www.upwork.com/freelance-jobs/content-moderation/

HTML freelance jobs

https://www.upwork.com/freelance-jobs/html/

HTML5 freelance jobs

https://www.upwork.com/freelance-jobs/html5/

InDesign work from home

https://www.upwork.com/freelance-jobs/adobe-indesign/

Infographic freelance jobs

https://www.upwork.com/freelance-jobs/infographic/

Infographic freelance jobs

https://www.upwork.com/freelance-jobs/infographics/

Informatica freelancing projects

https://www.upwork.com/freelance-jobs/informatica/

Information security freelance

https://www.upwork.com/o/jobs/browse/skill/information-security/

Instagram consultant jobs

https://www.upwork.com/o/jobs/browse/skill/instagram/

Instagram content creator job

https://www.upwork.com/o/jobs/browse/skill/instagram-marketing/

International ad posting jobs

https://www.upwork.com/freelance-jobs/ad-posting/

International online jobs for encoder

https://www.upwork.com/o/jobs/browse/skill/data-encoding/

Internet marketing jobs

https://www.upwork.com/o/jobs/browse/skill/internet-marketing/

Ionic framework jobs

https://www.upwork.com/freelance-jobs/ionic-framework/

Ionic freelancer

https://www.upwork.com/o/jobs/browse/skill/ionic-framework/

iPhone freelance projects

https://www.upwork.com/freelance-jobs/ios-development/

IT technician for hire

https://www.upwork.com/hire/computer-repair-technician/

Java freelance jobs online

https://www.upwork.com/freelance-jobs/java/

Java outsourcing jobs

https://www.upwork.com/o/jobs/browse/skill/java/

JavaScript freelance projects

https://www.upwork.com/freelance-jobs/javascript/

Job typing books into eBooks

https://www.upwork.com/o/jobs/browse/skill/ebooks/

Jobs for coders online

https://www.upwork.com/o/jobs/browse/?q=coding

Joomla freelance jobs

https://www.upwork.com/freelance-jobs/joomla/

Junior Java developer freelance

https://www.upwork.com/o/jobs/browse/skill/java/

Laravel freelance jobs

https://www.upwork.com/freelance-jobs/laravel-framework/

Lidar jobs online

https://www.upwork.com/o/jobs/browse/?q=lidar

Link building jobs online

https://www.upwork.com/o/jobs/browse/skill/link-building/

Linux system administrator freelance jobs

https://www.upwork.com/o/jobs/browse/skill/linux-system-administration/

Logo design work

https://www.upwork.com/freelance-jobs/logo/

Looking for digital artist

https://www.upwork.com/o/jobs/browse/skill/digital-art/

Looking for email marketing

https://www.upwork.com/freelance-jobs/email-marketing/

Machine learning online jobs

https://www.upwork.com/o/jobs/browse/skill/machine-learning/

Magento projects freelance

https://www.upwork.com/freelance-jobs/magento/

Mainframe freelance projects

https://www.upwork.com/o/jobs/browse/?q=mainframes

Managing Instagram accounts job

https://www.upwork.com/o/jobs/browse/skill/instagram/

Market researchers for hire

https://www.upwork.com/hire/marketing-researchers/

MATLAB online jobs

https://www.upwork.com/o/jobs/browse/skill/matlab/

MATLAB programming jobs online

https://www.upwork.com/freelance-jobs/matlab/

Maven freelance

https://www.upwork.com/o/jobs/browse/skill/maven/

Maya rigging freelance work

https://www.upwork.com/o/jobs/browse/?q=maya+rigging

Microsoft Access administration

https://www.upwork.com/freelance-jobs/microsoft-access/

Microsoft Dynamics AX freelance

https://www.upwork.com/o/jobs/browse/skill/microsoft-dynamics/

Microsoft Excel consulting jobs

https://www.upwork.com/o/jobs/browse/skill/microsoft-excel/

Microsoft Office jobs from home

https://www.upwork.com/o/jobs/browse/skill/microsoft-office/

Microsoft Word jobs

https://www.upwork.com/freelance-jobs/microsoft-word/

Mobile app testing jobs from home

https://www.upwork.com/o/jobs/browse/skill/mobile-app-testing/

MS Access jobs remote

https://www.upwork.com/o/jobs/browse/skill/microsoft-access/

MS Access programming jobs

https://www.upwork.com/freelance-jobs/microsoft-access-programming/

MS Excel online jobs

https://www.upwork.com/o/jobs/browse/c/software-development/skill/microsoft-excel/

MS Excel online jobs

https://www.upwork.com/o/jobs/browse/skill/microsoft-excel/

MS Office jobs online

https://www.upwork.com/o/jobs/browse/skill/microsoft-office/

MySQL freelance jobs

https://www.upwork.com/o/jobs/browse/skill/mysql/

Nav freelancer

https://www.upwork.com/o/jobs/browse/?q=dynamics+nav

NetSuite freelance jobs

https://www.upwork.com/freelance-jobs/netsuite/

Network analysis freelance

https://www.upwork.com/o/jobs/browse/skill/network-analysis/

Node JS developer freelance

https://www.upwork.com/freelance-jobs/node-js/

Node JS developer freelance

https://www.upwork.com/o/jobs/browse/skill/node-js/

Odesk php test

https://www.upwork.com/o/jobs/browse/skill/php/

Odesk wiki

https://www.upwork.com/freelance-jobs/wikipedia/

Odoo Upwork

https://www.upwork.com/freelance-jobs/odoo/

Online assistant

https://www.upwork.com/o/jobs/browse/c/admin-support/sc/personal-virtual-assistant/

Online audio engineering jobs

https://www.upwork.com/freelance-jobs/audio-engineering/

Online automation testing jobs

https://www.upwork.com/o/jobs/browse/?q=automation+selenium+testing

Online CAD drafting jobs

https://www.upwork.com/o/jobs/browse/skill/autocad/

Online CAD work

https://www.upwork.com/de/o/jobs/browse/skill/cad-design/

Online coding jobs in Java

https://www.upwork.com/freelance-jobs/java/

Online crypto jobs

https://www.upwork.com/o/jobs/browse/skill/cryptocurrency/

Online data editing jobs

https://www.upwork.com/o/jobs/browse/?q=data+editing

Online Excel work job

https://www.upwork.com/freelance-jobs/microsoft-excel/

Online freelance marketing

https://www.upwork.com/freelance-jobs/internet-marketing/

Online game review jobs

https://www.upwork.com/o/jobs/browse/?q=game+reviewer

Online game tester job openings

https://www.upwork.com/o/jobs/browse/skill/game-testing/

Online graphic design jobs

https://www.upwork.com/o/jobs/browse/skill/graphic-design/

Online IT projects jobs

https://www.upwork.com/o/jobs/browse/c/admin-support/sc/project-management/

Online jobs in digital marketing

https://www.upwork.com/o/jobs/browse/skill/internet-marketing/

Online marketing research jobs

https://www.upwork.com/freelance-jobs/market-research/

Online outsourcing work

https://www.upwork.com/freelance-jobs/it-outsourcing/

Online photo editing jobs

https://www.upwork.com/o/jobs/browse/skill/photo-editing/

Online PHP project work

https://www.upwork.com/freelance-jobs/php/

Online programming jobs

https://www.upwork.com/o/jobs/browse/?q=computer+programmer

Online project work in HTML

https://www.upwork.com/o/jobs/browse/skill/html/

Online projects on Python

https://www.upwork.com/o/jobs/browse/skill/python/

Online SEO projects jobs

https://www.upwork.com/o/jobs/browse/c/sales-marketing/sc/seo-search-engine-optimization/

Online SEO work projects

https://www.upwork.com/freelance-jobs/seo/

Online social media jobs

https://www.upwork.com/o/jobs/browse/skill/social-media-marketing/

Online software projects for developers

https://www.upwork.com/o/jobs/browse/c/web-mobile-software-dev/

Online system admin jobs

https://www.upwork.com/o/jobs/browse/skill/system-administration/

Oracle apps freelance work

https://www.upwork.com/o/jobs/browse/?q=oracle+apps.

Oracle EBS freelance jobs

https://www.upwork.com/o/jobs/browse/?q=ebs+oracle

Outsource projects jobs

https://www.upwork.com/o/jobs/browse/?q=outsourcing

Pay Per Click jobs from home

https://www.upwork.com/freelance-jobs/pay-per-click/

Pdf conversion jobs home

https://www.upwork.com/freelance-jobs/pdf-conversion/

Pdf conversion jobs online

https://www.upwork.com/o/jobs/browse/c/admin-support/skill/pdf-conversion/

Phalcon PHP jobs

https://www.upwork.com/o/jobs/browse/?q=phalcon+php

PhoneGap freelancer

https://www.upwork.com/o/jobs/browse/skill/phonegap/

Photoshop designer jobs online

https://www.upwork.com/freelance-jobs/adobe-photoshop/

Photoshop editing work at home

https://www.upwork.com/o/jobs/browse/skill/image-editing/

Pinterest freelance jobs

https://www.upwork.com/o/jobs/browse/skill/pinterest-marketing/

Planning freelance

https://www.upwork.com/o/jobs/browse/skill/strategic-planning/

PLC freelance

https://www.upwork.com/o/jobs/browse/skill/plc-programming/

PLC freelance work

https://www.upwork.com/o/jobs/browse/skill/plc-and-scada/

PLC freelance work

https://www.upwork.com/o/jobs/browse/skill/plc/

Podcast editing jobs

https://www.upwork.com/freelance-jobs/podcasting/

Power BI freelance jobs

https://www.upwork.com/o/jobs/browse/?q=microsoft+power+bi

Power BI freelance jobs

https://www.upwork.com/o/jobs/browse/skill/powerbi/

PowerPoint freelance

https://www.upwork.com/freelance-jobs/powerpoint/

PowerPoint jobs from home

https://www.upwork.com/o/jobs/browse/skill/microsoft-powerpoint/

PowerPoint jobs online

https://www.upwork.com/freelance-jobs/microsoft-powerpoint/

PowerShell freelance

https://www.upwork.com/freelance-jobs/powershell/

PowerShell freelance

https://www.upwork.com/o/jobs/browse/skill/microsoft-windows-powershell/

Presentation freelance

https://www.upwork.com/o/jobs/browse/skill/presentation-design/

Programming side jobs

https://www.upwork.com/o/jobs/browse/?q=server-side+programming

PSD to HTML remote jobs

https://www.upwork.com/o/jobs/browse/skill/psd-to-html/

Python developer freelance jobs

https://www.upwork.com/o/jobs/browse/skill/python/

Python online jobs

https://www.upwork.com/freelance-jobs/python/

QlikView freelance projects

https://www.upwork.com/o/jobs/browse/skill/qlikview/

Raspberry Pi freelancer

https://www.upwork.com/freelance-jobs/raspberry-pi/

React developer freelance

https://www.upwork.com/freelance-jobs/react-js/

React JS freelance work

https://www.upwork.com/o/jobs/browse/skill/react-js/

React native Upwork

https://www.upwork.com/freelance-jobs/react-native/

Repair and fix computer jobs

https://www.upwork.com/o/jobs/browse/skill/computer-repair/

Ruby on Rails freelance projects

https://www.upwork.com/o/jobs/browse/skill/ruby-on-rails/

Salesforce freelance

https://www.upwork.com/freelance-jobs/salesforce-app-development/

Salesforce freelance trainer

https://www.upwork.com/o/jobs/browse/?q=salesforce+training

SAP ABAP online jobs

https://www.upwork.com/o/jobs/browse/skill/sap-abap/

SAP ABAP projects online

https://www.upwork.com/freelance-jobs/sap-abap/

SAP BI freelance jobs

https://www.upwork.com/o/jobs/browse/?q=bi+sap

SAP BPC freelance

https://www.upwork.com/hire/sap-bpc-freelancers/

SAP freelancing projects

https://www.upwork.com/freelance-jobs/sap/

SAP Hana freelance projects

https://www.upwork.com/o/jobs/browse/skill/sap-hana/

SAP online jobs

https://www.upwork.com/o/jobs/browse/skill/sap/

SAP security freelance jobs

https://www.upwork.com/o/jobs/browse/?q=sap+security

SAS freelance

https://www.upwork.com/freelance-jobs/sas/

SCALA and big data

https://www.upwork.com/hiring/data/scala-hybrid-functionalobject-oriented-language-big-data/

SEO analyst freelance

https://www.upwork.com/o/jobs/browse/?q=analyst+seo

SEO freelance work from home

https://www.upwork.com/o/jobs/browse/c/sales-marketing/sc/seo-search-engine-optimization/

SEO jobs Upwork

https://www.upwork.com/o/jobs/browse/skill/seo/

SEO writing jobs

https://www.upwork.com/freelance-jobs/seo-writing/

SEO writing jobs online

https://www.upwork.com/o/jobs/browse/skill/seo-writing/

ServiceNow online jobs

https://www.upwork.com/o/jobs/browse/skill/servicenow/

Simple programming jobs

https://www.upwork.com/o/jobs/browse/?q=programming+simple

Sketchup freelancer

https://www.upwork.com/hire/google-sketchup-freelancers/

Sketchup jobs

https://www.upwork.com/freelance-jobs/google-sketchup/

Social media management freelance jobs

https://www.upwork.com/freelance-jobs/social-media-management/

Social media marketing freelance

https://www.upwork.com/freelance-jobs/social-media-marketing/

Software development projects freelance

https://www.upwork.com/o/jobs/browse/c/web-mobile-software-dev/

Software development work

https://www.upwork.com/o/jobs/browse/skill/agile-software-development/

Software testing projects for freelancers

https://www.upwork.com/o/jobs/browse/skill/software-testing/

Solidworks contract work

https://www.upwork.com/freelance-jobs/solidworks/

Solidworks drafting jobs from home

https://www.upwork.com/o/jobs/browse/skill/solidworks/

Splunk freelance jobs

https://www.upwork.com/o/jobs/browse/skill/splunk/

Squarespace consultant

https://www.upwork.com/hire/squarespace-developers/

Squarespace freelance

https://www.upwork.com/o/jobs/browse/skill/squarespace/

SSIS freelance jobs

https://www.upwork.com/o/jobs/browse/skill/ssis/

Startup consulting jobs

https://www.upwork.com/freelance-jobs/startup-consulting/

Symfony freelance jobs

https://www.upwork.com/o/jobs/browse/skill/symfony/

Tableau online jobs

https://www.upwork.com/o/jobs/browse/skill/tableau/

Tech writers wanted

https://www.upwork.com/freelance-jobs/technical-writing/

Technical support freelance jobs

https://www.upwork.com/freelance-jobs/technical-support/

Ui design freelance work

https://www.upwork.com/o/jobs/browse/skill/ui-design/

UI UX designer freelance

https://www.upwork.com/freelance-jobs/ux/

Unity 3d freelance work

https://www.upwork.com/o/jobs/browse/?q=c%23+unity+3d

Unity contract work

https://www.upwork.com/freelance-jobs/unity-3d/

Unreal engine freelance jobs

https://www.upwork.com/o/jobs/browse/skill/unreal/

Upwork Android test

https://www.upwork.com/o/jobs/browse/?q=android+app+testing

Upwork Android test

https://www.upwork.com/o/jobs/browse/?q=android+automated+testing

Upwork AWS

https://www.upwork.com/o/jobs/browse/?q=aws

Upwork AWS

https://www.upwork.com/o/jobs/browse/skill/amazon-ec2/

Upwork banner

https://www.upwork.com/o/jobs/browse/skill/banner-design/

Upwork C++

https://www.upwork.com/o/jobs/browse/skill/c-/

Upwork chatbot

https://www.upwork.com/o/jobs/browse/c/web-mobile-software-dev/sc/web-development/skill/chatbot-development/

Upwork customer service jobs

https://www.upwork.com/freelance-jobs/customer-support/

Upwork database

https://www.upwork.com/freelance-jobs/database/

Upwork database

https://www.upwork.com/o/jobs/browse/c/it-networking/sc/database-administration/

Upwork deep learning

https://www.upwork.com/freelance-jobs/deep-learning/

Upwork digital marketing

https://www.upwork.com/o/jobs/browse/?q=digital-marketing

Upwork Django developer

https://www.upwork.com/o/jobs/browse/?q=%22django+developer%22

Upwork editing jobs

https://www.upwork.com/freelance-jobs/editing/

Upwork Excel

https://www.upwork.com/freelance-jobs/excel/

Upwork front end developer

https://www.upwork.com/o/jobs/browse/?q=developer+frontend

Upwork full stack developer

https://www.upwork.com/o/jobs/browse/?q=developer+full+stack

Upwork Google

https://www.upwork.com/o/jobs/browse/skill/google-apps/

Upwork Java developer

https://www.upwork.com/o/jobs/browse/?q=java+programmer

Upwork JavaScript

https://www.upwork.com/hire/javascript-developers/

Upwork JavaScript

https://www.upwork.com/o/jobs/browse/skill/javascript/

Upwork payment gateway

https://www.upwork.com/o/jobs/browse/skill/payment-gateway-integration/

Upwork R programming

https://www.upwork.com/o/jobs/browse/?q=programming+r

Upwork Salesforce jobs

https://www.upwork.com/o/jobs/browse/?q=administrator+salesforce

Upwork Salesforce jobs

https://www.upwork.com/o/jobs/browse/?q=crm%2c+salesforce

Upwork social media marketing

https://www.upwork.com/o/jobs/browse/c/sales-marketing/sc/smm-social-media-marketing/

Upwork software

https://www.upwork.com/freelance-jobs/desktop-applications/

Upwork Unity developer

https://www.upwork.com/o/jobs/browse/skill/unity3d/

Upwork web design

https://www.upwork.com/freelance-jobs/responsive-web-design/

Upwork Wiki

https://www.upwork.com/freelance-jobs/wiki/

Upwork WooCommerce

https://www.upwork.com/freelance-jobs/woocommerce/

VB NET online jobs

https://www.upwork.com/o/jobs/browse/skill/vb-net/

VBA freelance work

https://www.upwork.com/freelance-jobs/vba/

VBA work

https://www.upwork.com/o/jobs/browse/skill/vba/

VFX work from home

https://www.upwork.com/freelance-jobs/vfx-animation/

Video animation jobs

https://www.upwork.com/freelance-jobs/video-animation/

Video editing projects online

https://www.upwork.com/freelance-jobs/video-editing/

Video game streaming jobs

https://www.upwork.com/o/jobs/browse/?q=game+streaming+video

Visual Basic freelance work

https://www.upwork.com/o/jobs/browse/skill/visual-basic/

Vuejs freelance

https://www.upwork.com/freelance-jobs/vue-js/

Web content writing projects

https://www.upwork.com/freelance-jobs/content-writing/

Web design online work

https://www.upwork.com/o/jobs/browse/skill/responsive-web-design/

Web design projects freelance

https://www.upwork.com/o/jobs/browse/skill/web-design/

Web design work

https://www.upwork.com/freelance-jobs/web-design/

Web designer freelance website

https://www.upwork.com/freelance-jobs/web-design/

Web research companies

https://www.upwork.com/o/jobs/browse/skill/internet-research/

Web research jobs

https://www.upwork.com/freelance-jobs/internet-research/

Web scraping jobs online

https://www.upwork.com/freelance-jobs/web-scraping/

Webgl freelance

https://www.upwork.com/o/jobs/browse/skill/webgl/

Website content moderator jobs

https://www.upwork.com/o/jobs/browse/skill/content-moderation/

Website developer jobs online

https://www.upwork.com/o/jobs/browse/c/web-mobile-software-dev/sc/web-development/

Website developer jobs online

https://www.upwork.com/o/jobs/browse/skill/website-development/

Webstore com jobs

https://www.upwork.com/o/jobs/browse/skill/amazon-webstore/

Wiki Upwork

https://www.upwork.com/o/jobs/browse/skill/wiki/

Wix designer jobs

https://www.upwork.com/freelance-jobs/wix/

Wix developer jobs

https://www.upwork.com/o/jobs/browse/skill/wix/

WordPress freelance jobs

https://www.upwork.com/freelance-jobs/wordpress/

WordPress freelance jobs plugin

https://www.upwork.com/freelance-jobs/wordpress-plugin/

Work as a graphic designer online

https://www.upwork.com/freelance-jobs/graphic-design/

Work in NET

https://www.upwork.com/o/jobs/browse/skill/asp-net/

XML freelance jobs

https://www.upwork.com/freelance-jobs/xml/

YouTube subtitle job

https://www.upwork.com/o/jobs/browse/?q=subtitle+youtube

YouTube video editor jobs

https://www.upwork.com/freelance-jobs/youtube/

Zapier freelancer

https://www.upwork.com/freelance-jobs/zapier/

ZOHO developer jobs

https://www.upwork.com/freelance-jobs/zoho-creator/

ZOHO freelancer

https://www.upwork.com/o/jobs/browse/skill/zoho-crm/

Zoom freelance

https://www.upwork.com/o/jobs/browse/skill/zoom-video-conferencing/

17 UPWORK IT ROLES BY POPULARITY (GLOBAL)

This shows IT Roles by Internet traffic in descending order. Which IT activities are the most popular?

Freelance web developer, freelance videographer, freelance it jobs, internet marketing jobs, online graphic design jobs, freelance social media jobs, freelance web developer jobs, freelance video editing jobs, graphic design work, freelance 3d modeling, online assistant, online social media jobs, data science freelance, freelance blog writer, freelance data analysis, freelance data scientist, freelance web design jobs, hire iOS developer, online programming jobs, admin online, freelance cad work, freelance graphic design work, freelance iOS developer, podcast editing jobs, social media marketing freelance, freelance virtual assistant jobs, GIS freelance, online photo editing jobs, programming side jobs, salesforce freelance, SketchUp jobs, WordPress freelance jobs, YouTube video editor jobs, excel freelance jobs, freelance AutoCAD jobs, freelance business analyst, freelance SEO jobs, Upwork wiki, animation work, freelance content creator, freelance copywriter website, freelance JavaScript jobs, SEO writing jobs, 3d animation work, 3d architectural visualization freelance jobs, Angular freelance jobs, Angular freelance jobs, Azure freelance jobs, Delphi freelance work, freelance 2d animation jobs, freelance automation testing jobs, freelance data analytics projects, freelance objective C, freelance social media designer, freelance social media marketing manager, game development freelance projects, Informatica freelancing projects, MS Access programming jobs, NetSuite freelance jobs, simple programming jobs, SketchUp freelancer, Webgl freelance, Wix designer jobs, xml freelance jobs, 3d freelance jobs online, Arduino freelance jobs, ASP NET freelance work, blockchain freelance projects, Django freelance projects, excel spreadsheet freelance work, freelance CNC programming, freelance code work, freelance communications jobs, freelance embedded programmer, freelance IT projects, freelance

SharePoint developer jobs, freelance Six Sigma jobs, freelance system administrator jobs, freelancer content marketing, Google AdWords work from home, Google Analytics Upwork, hire Etsy expert, Ionic framework jobs, IT technician for hire, JavaScript freelance projects, Odoo Upwork, online marketing research jobs, PhoneGap freelancer, PowerPoint freelance, python online jobs, react native Upwork, Scala and big data, Startup consulting jobs, UI UX designer freelance, Unity 3d freelance work, Upwork chatbot, Upwork WooCommerce, web design work, Zapier freelancer, ZOHO developer jobs, 2d animation work from home, Adobe Photoshop freelance work, AdSense jobs online, After Effects freelance work, Bash scripting jobs, BI freelance jobs, data collection freelancer, digital marketing freelance projects, Dynamics CRM freelance jobs, Facebook Ads Manager freelance, freelance AdWords, freelance Angular 2 developer, freelance automation projects, freelance Catia, freelance content developer, freelance CSS designer, freelance development consultant, freelance GIS jobs online, freelance Hadoop developer, freelance help desk jobs, freelance HTML5 game developer, freelance IT support jobs, freelance sysadmin jobs, freelancer MIS jobs, Hadoop freelance jobs, Hadoop freelance jobs, hire Facebook marketing expert, looking for email marketing, Microsoft Access administration, nav freelancer, online data editing jobs, online outsourcing work, online PHP project work, Raspberry Pi freelancer, Salesforce freelance trainer, SAP ABAP projects online, SAS freelance, social media management freelance jobs, Splunk freelance jobs, Upwork customer service jobs, Upwork deep learning, Upwork Django developer, Upwork editing jobs, Upwork google, VBA freelance work, video animation jobs, video editing projects online, web designer freelance website, web scraping jobs online, WordPress freelance jobs plugin, 3d conversion jobs, 3d outsourcing jobs, Ansys freelance, ArcGIS online jobs, blender 3d freelance jobs, business development consultant freelance, CNC programming from home, ColdFusion freelance projects, core php jobs, d3 JS freelance, DBA freelance work, digital marketing Upwork profile, DTP jobs work from home, Dynamics AX freelance jobs, Dynamics Nav freelance jobs, Flash animation freelance work, freelance database jobs, freelance embedded software developer, freelance Excel consultant, freelance front end web developer jobs, freelance Java programming work, freelance machine learning project, freelance penetration testing jobs, freelance PL SQL developer, freelance tech work, freelance web design jobs for beginners, Fusion 360 freelance, game developer Upwork, hardware freelancer, hire PhoneGap developer, home based content moderator, InDesign work from home, infographic freelance jobs, infographic freelance jobs, Java freelance jobs online, Joomla freelance jobs, Magento projects freelance, MATLAB programming jobs online, network analysis freelance, online Excel work job, online SEO work projects, Pay Per Click jobs from home, pdf conversion jobs home, Phalcon PHP jobs, photoshop designer jobs online, PLC freelance, PowerShell freelance, PowerShell freelance, SAP BPC freelance, Squarespace consultant, unreal engine freelance jobs, Upwork banner, Upwork Excel, Upwork front end developer, VFX work from home, website content moderator jobs, 3d design jobs online, 3d design jobs online, 3d visualizer freelance jobs, ABAP freelance opportunities, Adobe InDesign jobs, AI freelance jobs, app promotion jobs, app testing jobs online, ArcGIS freelance jobs, ArcGIS freelance jobs, build website freelance, C# online jobs, CAE freelance jobs, computer vision freelance jobs, content writing freelance work, copywriting work, Corel Draw jobs online, Creo freelance jobs, data encoder online, data visualization freelance, deep learning freelance jobs, DevOps freelance jobs, ERP freelance jobs, ERP freelancer, Ethereum freelance jobs, ETL freelance jobs, ETL freelance jobs, freelance animation projects, freelance AutoCAD jobs from home, freelance big data engineer, freelance C++ programming jobs, freelance computer jobs from home, freelance cyber security jobs, freelance database design, freelance database developer jobs, freelance digital marketing services, freelance documentation, freelance ecommerce jobs, freelance ecommerce manager, freelance eLearning jobs, freelance embedded software engineer, freelance front end developer work, freelance Fusion 360 jobs, freelance HTML coding jobs, freelance jobs for Selenium testing, freelance marketing research jobs, freelance media production, freelance mobile app testing, freelance MS Access jobs, freelance MS Project, freelance newsletter writer, freelance photo editing online, freelance product developer, freelance Python developer jobs, freelance rendering jobs, freelance reporting services, freelance research projects, freelance system developer, freelance technical writer wanted, freelance Unity programmer, freelance webmaster, freelancer chatbot, game developer needed, Golang freelance jobs, information security freelance, international ad posting jobs, international online jobs for encoder, Java outsourcing jobs, job typing books into eBooks, logo design work, market researchers for hire, MATLAB online jobs, Maya rigging freelance work, Microsoft Word jobs, MS Access jobs remote, Node JS developer freelance, Node JS developer freelance, Odesk wiki, online audio engineering jobs, online CAD drafting jobs, online freelance marketing, online IT projects jobs, online jobs in digital marketing, online project work in HTML, online system admin jobs, outsource projects jobs, Pinterest freelance jobs, planning freelance, QlikView freelance projects, React JS freelance work, repair and fix computer jobs, SAP BI freelance jobs, SAP Hana freelance projects, SAP online jobs, SEO analyst freelance, SEO writing jobs online, ServiceNow online jobs, software development work, Squarespace freelance, Symfony freelance jobs, tech writers wanted, technical support freelance jobs, Unity contract work, Upwork Android test, Upwork C++, Upwork database, Upwork digital marketing, Upwork JavaScript, Upwork Unity developer, web content writing projects, Wiki Upwork, Wix developer jobs, Zoom freelance, 2d animation jobs freelance, 3d rendering jobs for freelancers, 3ds Max designer jobs, 3ds Max modeling jobs, Android app development online jobs, Android app development online jobs, Angular 2 freelance jobs, ASP NET MVC freelance jobs, Autodesk Fusion jobs, Autodesk Inventor freelance projects, Autodesk Inventor work from home, automation freelance, automation freelance, AWS freelance work, backend freelance, Bitcoin freelance, Blender 3d freelance, blockchain developer freelance, business objects freelance jobs, CAD design from home, Catia freelance jobs, Clickfunnels freelancer, Clojure freelance jobs, ColdFusion freelance work, companies looking for video production, computer repair work, computer technician for hire, core Java freelance jobs, data mining freelance, Dot NET freelance jobs, Dot NET freelancer, editor needed for YouTube, email marketing Upwork, Facebook API freelancer, forum posting jobs, freelance 3d printing jobs, freelance 3d projects, freelance academic writing jobs online, freelance admin jobs online, freelance Android application developer, freelance Angular, freelance audio editing jobs, freelance audio jobs, freelance business development jobs, freelance CAD designer jobs, freelance cloud consultant, freelance CNC work, freelance computer engineer, freelance data capturing, freelance data collection jobs, freelance data jobs, freelance email copywriter, freelance email designer, freelance embedded projects, freelance Facebook marketing, freelance Flash animation jobs, freelance game designer, freelance GIS specialist, freelance graphic jobs online, freelance help desk support, freelance Internet researcher, freelance iPhone app developer, freelance IT solutions, freelance Java J2ee projects, freelance jobs machine learning, freelance jobs PowerPoint presentation, freelance Joomla jobs, freelance Linux, freelance network technician, freelance operations consultant, freelance PHP MySQL programmer, freelance PHP MySQL programmer, freelance PMP, freelance podcast editor jobs, freelance process engineer, freelance product development, freelance product manager jobs, freelance QA testing projects, freelance R programming, freelance React developer, freelance report writing jobs, freelance RPA, freelance Ruby programmer, freelance SEO content writing jobs, freelance SharePoint consultants, freelance social media content creator, freelance SQL server developer, freelance Startup jobs, freelance statistical analysis, freelance statistical analysis, freelance Tableau consulting, freelance technical support jobs, freelance telecom jobs, freelance usability, freelance video game designer, freelance web application projects, freelance web content, freelance web developer wanted, game streaming jobs, Google ad jobs online, graphic designer needed for logo, graphic work online, hire Java programmer online, hire Wix developer, HTML freelance jobs, HTML5 freelance jobs, Instagram consultant jobs, Instagram content creator job, Ionic freelancer, iPhone freelance projects, jobs for coders online, junior Java developer freelance, Laravel freelance jobs, Lidar jobs online, link building jobs online, Linux system administrator freelance jobs, looking for digital artist, machine learning online jobs, mainframe freelance projects, managing Instagram accounts job, Maven freelance, Microsoft Dynamics AX freelance, Microsoft Excel consulting jobs, Microsoft Office jobs from home, mobile app testing jobs from home, MS Excel online jobs, MS Excel online jobs, MS Office jobs online, MySQL freelance jobs, Odesk PHP test, online automation testing jobs, online cad work, online coding jobs in Java, online crypto jobs, online game review jobs, online game tester job openings, online projects on Python, online SEO projects jobs, online software projects for developers, Oracle apps freelance work, Oracle EBS freelance jobs, pdf conversion jobs online, Photoshop editing work at home, PLC freelance work, PLC freelance work, Power BI freelance jobs, PowerPoint jobs from home, PowerPoint jobs online, presentation freelance, PSD to HTML remote jobs, Python developer freelance jobs, React developer freelance, Ruby on Rails freelance projects, SAP ABAP online jobs, SAP freelancing projects, SAP security freelance jobs, SEO freelance work from home, SEO jobs Upwork, software development projects freelance, software testing projects for freelancers, Solidworks contract work, Solidworks drafting jobs from home, SSIS freelance jobs, Tableau online jobs, UI design freelance work, Upwork AWS, Upwork full stack developer, Upwork Java developer, Upwork payment gateway, Upwork R programming, Upwork Salesforce jobs, Upwork social media marketing, Upwork software, Upwork web design, VB NET online jobs, VBA work, video game streaming jobs, Visual Basic freelance work, Vuejs freelance, web design online work, web design projects freelance, web research companies, web research jobs, website developer jobs online, website developer jobs online, webstore com jobs, work as a graphic designer online, work in NET, YouTube subtitle job, ZOHO freelancer

18 GLOBAL JOB WEBSITES BY POPULARITY

The Job Websites listed below are ranked by Internet traffic.

Job websites selected in this book are based on sites that provide English IT Role links.

indeed.com

linkedin.com

glassdoor.com

ziprecruiter.com

seek.com.au

simplyhired.com

monster.com

glassdoor.co.uk/

glassdoor.ca

jora.com

fiverr.com

flexjobs.com

payscale.com

upwork.com

glassdoor.com.au

behance.net

toptal.com

freelancer.com

taskrabbit.com

guru.com

19 IT CAREER DIGITAL RESOURCES – 1500+ IT ROLES CHECKLIST AND 1800+ IT ROLE LINKS

The following links allow you to process your Job Search faster.

Create a shortlist of suitable IT roles from a list of over 1500 and export them as text.

Find which job website list your suitable IT Roles and link directly to the career, job, project or contract listings.

Book Resources Homepage

https://itjobsformula.com/

1500+ Roles in IT checklist. Export your suitable IT Roles list

https://itjobsformula.com/jobs/

250+ Seek Roles in IT with Salaries and Links

https://itjobsformula.com/seek/

300+ Indeed International Roles in IT with Links

https://itjobsformula.com/indeed/

300+ Indeed UK Roles in IT with Links

https://itjobsformula.com/indeedcouk/

350+ Freelancer Roles in IT with Links

https://itjobsformula.com/freelancer/

200 Zip Recruiter Roles in IT with Links

https://itjobsformula.com/ziprecruiter/

500+ Upwork Roles in IT with Links

https://itjobsformula.com/upwork/

20 CONCLUSION

The knowledge from this book should help you search and find more IT job opportunities that can be actioned quickly. Processes can be reused for contract, part time, full time and project work. IT jobs also have the benefit of remote work options. IT can be applied to most industries. Who else could benefit from the knowledge of the IT industry jobs demand and IT job opportunities? Digital tools at https://itjobsformula.com/ can help speed up your productivity to get your dream IT career.

ABOUT THE AUTHOR

Who Is Matthew Bulat And Why Should I Listen To Him?

Matthew Bulat is an expert in IT Jobs whose accomplishments include:

Education:

• Master of Engineering Technology

Work History:

• University IT Lecturer covering 14 subjects

• 12 years as Australian Computer Society NQ Chapter Chairman

• 10 years' experience managing IT systems for Federal and Local government

Awards, Titles, and Designations:

• Senior Member Australian Computer Society, Certified Professional

• Platinum Level Microsoft Virtual Academy

Personal Info:

• 60,000 keywords reviewed for IT Roles

• Tracking IT jobs market for 6 years

• Runs a global website with users in 230+ countries

• Over 1 million users per year to website

• Created IT and Business skills analysis web pages.

So as you can see, Matthew Bulat is uniquely qualified to help you understand everything you need to know about IT Jobs!